DATE DUE

AP 17 '95			
DE 22 '95			
NO 24			
AP 22 '02			
MY 22 '02			
JE 11 '03			

Effective Learning
Into a New ERA

of related interest

Teacher Appraisal: A Nationwide Approach
Edited by Alan Evans and John Tomlinson
ISBN 1 85302 508 9

Directors of Education - Facing Reform
Tony Bush, Maurice Kogan and Tony Bush
ISBN 1 85302 506 2

Evaluation as Policymaking:
Introducing Evaluation into a National
Decentralised Educational System
Edited by Marit Granheim, Maurice Kogan and Ulf Lundgren
ISBN 1 85302 515 1

Caught in the Act:
Assessment of Children with Special Needs
H Chasty and J Frierl
ISBN 1 85302 096 6

Effective Learning
Into a New ERA

Edited by Tim Everton, Peter Mayne and Steve White

Jessica Kingsley Publishers
London

First published in 1990 by
Jessica Kingsley Publishers Ltd
118 Pentonville Road
London N1 9JN

British Library Cataloguing in Publication Data
is available

Printed and bound in Great Britain by
Biddles Ltd, Guildford and King's Lynn

Contents

PART III: MONITORING AND ACCOUNTABILITY
Evaluating effective learning

Foreword

The 1990s will be a hectic and demanding decade for all of us who are concerned with improving the quality of effective learning in our schools. Significant additions to the responsibilities of governors, a changing emphasis in the role of local education authorities (LEAs); the gradual introduction of a national curriculum with the publication of national assessment outcomes; changing accountabilities at a time of teacher shortage; uncertain demography; and above all a huge requirement for training for teachers and for governors to enable them to adjust to their new roles and responsibilities - all signify a challenge for the organisation of available time of lay and professional partners in the education service in the United Kingdom.

This process is a direct outcome of a most radical piece of educational legislation which at one level has introduced the concept of market forces and interinstitutional competition into an education service which was growing rapidly to appreciate the value of interinstitutional collaboration and cooperation to maximise the utilisation of the skills and resources of families of schools. We must all be on our guard to ensure that the impetus of recent years in this direction is not lost as we seek as a service to respond to the demands of the 1988 Act.

It is difficult for any of the partners easily to predict the shape of the education service by the end of the century as we come to grips with implementation of the legislation at a time of unpredictable demography and resources.

How important it is therefore that lay and professional members of the partnership should take time out to reflect on the direction in which they wish the service to go, while implementing the practical requirements of the legislation and keeping very much to the forefront of their minds the paramount necessity that those children and young people who are in the system should not be adversely affected by the mechanics of change.

The Curriculum Association has a well-deserved reputation for keeping this objective firmly on the agenda and in this volume has brought together a wide range of international contributors who have addressed a number of key issues with an eye to the future which will do much to keep readers aware as they struggle with their day to day tasks. The partners in the service must be clear about the outcomes they seek to achieve for the benefit of young people in their various contributions to the development of the education service in the next decade.

Keith Wood-Allum, Director of Education, Leicestershire

Acknowledgements

The Leicester 1989 Conference of the Curriculum Association, 'Effective Learning - into the 1990s', was planned and organised by members of the Leicestershire Branch of the Association. Their energy, enthusiasm and imagination is illustrated in the wide ranging ideas and analysis contained within this book. The aims of the Association to involve all sectors of education in common pursuit of school and curriculum research and improvement have been vigorously promoted and appreciative thanks to the planning committee of the conference are recorded here.

Barry Day	Vice Principal, Mundella Community College, Leicester
Chris Davis	Headteacher, Queniborough C E Primary School, Leicester
Alan Dodds	Senior Teacher, Groby Community College, Leicester
Tim Everton	Senior Lecturer in Education, Leicester University
Peter Mayne	Leicestershire Advisory and Inspection Service
Margaret Ramsdale	(Treasurer) - Co-director of the Leicester Compact
Rick Ramsdale	King Edward VII School, Coalville, Leicester
Glyn Rawlins	Deputy Head, Trinity School, Northampton
Steve White	(Chairman) - Headteacher, Rushey Mead School, Leicester

Thanks should also be extended to all those who contributed to the conference, including members of the Thinking Skills Network.

Preface

This book has been developed from a highly successful conference of the Curriculum Association held at the University of Leicester in the spring of 1989. It represents the latest in a series of publications recording Association conferences each one of which has managed to capture a flavour of the contemporary scene in curriculum affairs.[1]

The Leicester conference was held at a significant time for anyone with an involvement and interest in curriculum. The Education Reform Act had passed onto the statute books just six months earlier. The outline form and structure of the National Curriculum for England and Wales was in place. It was clear that there were implications for Northern Ireland and Scotland. There was also no doubt that the curriculum plans were part of a longer agenda for educational reform. Curriculum by legislative decree had been placed in the widest possible context. We were also aware that government was reluctant, even amongst those favourable to parts of the proposal, to enter into a debate about the way in which the plans would be implemented. One of the most dispiriting aspects of the national policy making for the curriculum has been the secrecy with which ideas are formulated and alternatives considered. During the weekend in which this Preface was written the educational press had given two more sadly familiar examples. HMI responsible for religious education formally independent of DES, have been denied publication of a subject report in the very helpful 'Curriculum Matters' series. And Secretary of State John McGregor has announced a seemingly divisive arrangement linking GCSE and the National Curriculum after months of rumour and reports of bureaucratic infighting. No doubt the surveillance by certain political pressure groups has been a significant part of this process. How much more healthy an open and democratic debate would have been. Organisations such as the Curriculum Association (registered as a charity and non political) have an increasingly important role in providing a forum for public discussion in the 1990s. A number of the contributors to this volume have therefore chosen to examine critically aspects of the new proposals. Equally, however, the imperatives of government legislation should not overly detract attention from underlying pedagogical and organisational issues. Indeed it can be argued that it is just at moments like these that such concerns should be to the forefront. More than half the contributors address concerns that transcend the implications of the Education Reform Act. The editors are to be congratulated on striking such a healthy balance.

Bob Moon
Chair, Curriculum Association
January 1990

Note

1. See, for example, Richards, C. ed. (1979) *Power and the Curriculum*, Driffield: Nafferton Press; Galton, M. and Moon, B. eds. (1983) *Changing Schools ... Changing Curriculum*, London: Harper and Row.

Part I

CONTEXTS AND FUTURES:
Effective learning after the
Education Reform Act

Introduction

'...there are many things we treasure in education which are not actually encouraged by the new legislation but which are nevertheless not illegal.'

Joan Sallis

The new legislation reflects a societal and political climate in which we are required to view education as a market place. Schools are encouraged to compete with each other and have little incentive to share good practice. Those aspects of the Education Reform Act concerned with 'opting out' are seen by many as a blatant attack on the comprehensive system of education and on the power of local education authorities. All this suggests a discouraging context for the future, but one in which there is a pressing need to respond to Joan Sallis's more optimistic analysis. How can we continue to hang on to what we value in the aftermath of recent legislation, and how, in the new climate, do we continue the vital process of promoting effective learning in our schools? These are the questions addressed by the four contributors to this opening section, all of whom are concerned with the future of education in the context of the new legislation.

According to Michael Armstrong, effective learning at any age entails an 'active engagement ... a ceaseless struggle with *meaning*, a prolonged effort of mind to change and reshape experience ...'. But reference to the quality of meaning does not appear among any of the attainment targets of the national curriculum. How can we expect classroom practice to be geared to encouraging and fostering meaning when meaning is neither officially targeted nor publicly assessed? The responsibility for restoring meaning to its place at the centre of the educational enterprise must lie with teachers. In the opening chapter, Michael Armstrong vividly explains how teachers can reconstruct the national curriculum so that it gives expression to a more dynamic understanding of the relationship between form and meaning.

Joan Sallis is particularly concerned with the effect of legislation on schools and their governors and with how schools make their decisions. The Education Act of 1986 requires 'the creation of governing bodies balanced in composition, sharing decisions about school life, working openly, communicating with parents and the wider community, and within themselves affording equal rights to all groups'. This should not be confused by teachers with the pressure towards a market-driven service associated by many people with some of the legislation of the 1988 Act. Indeed the 1986 Act provides the structures which can help schools implement the later legislation with proper regard for the values that all those concerned with the quality of education are anxious to preserve. It provides schools with the opportunity to build some powerful partnerships with parents and governors for the protection of confident teaching and effective learning. Teachers, and particularly head teachers, must be positive about these developments and see governors and parents as their allies in battles for the future of education. Schools need these new friends in a situation where local education authorities may no longer be able to offer teachers the kind of support and protection to which they have been used.

The role of the local education authority will inevitably change in the light of the new legislation. Indeed Brian Simon views the ERA as primarily an attack on local government and its control of local school systems. He sees the major objective being the destruction of the existing system of comprehensive primary and secondary education and echoes Sallis's fear that education will change from a public service meeting needs to a free market responding to demands. The long-term strategy for this transformation is the establishment of opted-out or grant-maintained schools and the foundation of city technology colleges. Simon calls on the local education authority to take the lead in defence of their systems but, like Sallis, recognises the need for partnerships with other groups if values are to be protected and battles won. The aim must be to retain control of schools for the whole of the local community and to resist attempts to set individual groups of parents at loggerheads with each other.

Tim Brighouse takes up the theme of the changing role of the local education authorities. Through the implementation of local management of schools, they may even be involved in constructing a system in which they may ultimately have no role at all. To survive they must avoid too many schools opting out since each one that does increases the burden of central overheads for those that remain and the likelihood of a domino effect. Brighouse has sound advice for local education authorities in this respect. They need to get the details of local management of schools (LMS) and all other parts of the legislation right; they need to produce a system of handing money over that is better than a central government system; and they need to provide schools and teachers with an umbrella to shield them from the mind-numbing bombardment of change. At least if local education authorities do that, schools may count the cost as well as the advantages of opting out. The system might then hold out until the next major Reform Act which will come a lot sooner than the 45 years separating the Butler and Baker Acts.

A final theme running through all these chapters in this first part of the book is that of *communication*. The promotion of effective learning and improved communication need to go hand in hand. For Armstrong this implies teachers attending to children's meanings before attempting to intervene and offer guidance in the classroom. For Sallis it means teachers communicating to parents and governors all the good things going on in schools, winning their hearts and minds for the battle to preserve and share these things. For Simon it means communicating to politicians that education is a complex process, and that the crucial tasks of making teaching and learning more effective must remain in the hands of teachers. For Brighouse it means communicating to anyone willing to listen the principles on which we wish to see the future of education based. Indeed perhaps the next Education Reform Act will be a much shorter piece of legislation beginning with a statement of these principles so that people can see what we are actually trying to do and a clear agenda is set for achieving effective learning for our pupils in the twenty-first century.

Chapter 1

Does the national curriculum rest on a mistake?

Michael Armstrong

Midway through the first report of the National Curriculum English Working Group, austerely entitled *English for Ages 5 to 11*, the patient reader will come across a curious paragraph, the significance of which has so far escaped attention. (The paragraph in question is numbered 10.19; official thinking always seems to come in numbered paragraphs, naturally enough, for they suit its prescriptive purpose.) It reads as follows:

> 'The best writing is vigorous, committed, honest and interesting. We have not included these qualities in our attainment targets because they cannot be mapped onto levels. Even so, all good classroom practice will be geared to encouraging and fostering these vital qualities.'

In the second report of the working group, *English for Ages 5 to 16*, this paragraph is numbered 17.31. It is unchanged except that the words 'attainment targets' have been altered to 'statements of attainment'!

Now vigour, commitment, honesty and interest are all qualities of meaning, among its most important qualities one might suppose. The report appears to be arguing, then, that quality of meaning is not to be included among the attainment targets for writing in the newly prescribed national English curriculum. A study of the attainment targets themselves confirms this impression.

The odd thing is that elsewhere the report goes out of its way to emphasise the importance of meaning in determining the shape of English. It insists that 'teachers provide the greatest encouragement for children to communicate in writing when they respond more to the content of what is written than to (errors of letter formation, spelling and composition)' (10.13). It argues that 'it is a prerequisite of successful teaching of reading ... that (whenever techniques are taught) ... meaning should always be in the foreground' (9.4). It endorses the view that 'where children are given responsibility they are placed in situations where it becomes important for them to communicate - to discuss, to negotiate, to converse - with their fellows, with the staff, with other adults. And of necessity they are likely to develop oral skills' (prefatory quotation to Chapter 8). Throughout the report teachers are urged to show 'respect for an interest in the learner's language, culture, thought and intentions,' that is to say in the learner's meanings. It comes as a shock then to discover here in the middle of Chapter 10 that the very authors who are about to define the first attainment in writing as 'a growing ability to construct and convey meaning in written language' have chosen, with no undue sense of discomfort, to exclude from consideration as part, if not the chief part, of that attainment the quality of meaning constructed or conveyed.

The significance of this exclusion can scarcely be exaggerated. The attainment targets represent the driving force of the national curriculum. It is these targets that determine the programmes of study and the means of assessment. It is on these that teachers, parents, employers and governments, to say nothing of the children themselves, are expected to focus their attention. If in evaluating children's progress teachers are not required to attend to children's meanings, those meanings will lose their value. It can only be an illusion to suppose that classroom practice will be geared to encouraging and fostering meaning when meaning is neither officially targeted nor publicly assessed.

How is the inconsistency to be explained? Why should the English Working Group so strenuously promote meaning and so readily discount its assessment? To understand the Group's dilemma it is necessary to bear in mind the ideological conflicts that have helped to motivate the national curriculum as laid down in the 1988 Education Act. The issue concerns the curriculum as a whole and not only the teaching of English. The English Working Group is far from alone in its commitment to meaning. In one way or another each of the Working Groups to have reported so far (mathematics, science, technology, English) has been anxious to endorse the progressive assumption that children's thought is meaningful and that it is by attending to children's meanings that teachers most effectively promote learning. The problem is that progressive assumptions are unwelcome to the present Government and its advisers. It is not surprising, therefore, to find that the national curriculum is impervious to meaning as the working groups understand it. The curriculum outlined in the red-covered Consultation Document of 1987 and incorporated in the Education Act of 1988 is viewed exclusively from above, in terms of knowledge acquired, instruction received, subject matter handed down. No attention is paid to the significance of knowledge in children's present lives, to the way in which it serves their purposes, challenges their experience, and is reproduced and transformed in their practice. The impassive surface of departmental prose barely conceals the unspoken premise that the meanings which children construct, whether in literature, science or mathematics, are of little account. Knowledge has first to be acquired; only then can it be put to use. 'School education,' as the conservative philosopher Michael Oakeshott once memorably put it, 'is learning to speak before one has anything significant to say.'

Torn between their progressive instincts as experienced teachers and the constraints of their brief as architects of a conservative national curriculum, the working groups have chosen to contradict themselves rather than to confront the political challenge implicit in any attempt to impose a curriculum on schools by force of law. So while the context in which the working groups place their recommendations consistently argues the case for attending to meaning, the recommendations themselves ignore it, at least as far as the all-important attainment targets are concerned. Perhaps the hope is that teachers will look behind the letter of the recommendations to the spirit that informs them. It is another illusion. As consultative reports follow working group reports and draft orders follow consultative reports, so, little by little, the underlying argument disappears and we are left with bare recommendations which finally assume the status of law. The numbered paragraphs give way to the Ten Commandments.

Of all the working groups to have reported so far, only the mathematics Group, in its ill-fated attempt to develop a set of attainment targets specifically devoted to the practical application of mathematics, has made any serious attempt to find a way of evaluating children's meanings that might be consistent with the concept of attainment targets as defined in the Education Act and elaborated in the TGAT Report. Predictably, the National Curriculum Council refused to endorse this attempt which exposed all too effectively the limitations of attainment targets as determinants of the curriculum.

As the failure of the working groups to address the problem of meaning in relation to the national curriculum becomes clear, so the responsibility for restoring meaning to its place at the centre of the educational enterprise will pass to the teachers in the schools. Fortunately, one of the best things about *English for Ages 5 to 11*, for all its inconsistency, is the way in which it helps teachers to clarify their responsibility. It is the only one of the working group reports to recognise, explicitly, that any effective curriculum has to be grounded in a theory of the child no less than a theory of the subject. Surprisingly perhaps, in view of its chairman's reputation as co-editor of the Black Papers in the late 1960s and early 1970s, the report is at pains to endorse one of the Plowden Report's most notorious and unguarded maxims: 'no advances in policy ... have their desired effect unless they are in harmony with the nature of the child'. It is a pity that the authors offer us no sketch of what they suppose the child's nature to be, but the outlines of such a sketch are easy enough to reconstruct from the subsequent argument. Roughly the theory runs as follows.

Effective learning at any age entails an 'active engagement', to adopt the Report's own phraseology, in the various practices that define our culture, whether these are construed as subjects, areas of experience, forms of thought or intellectual traditions.

Let us consider the practice of narrative. 'Narrative,' we are told, 'has been described as a primary act of mind; children construct the world through story.' In as much as children are able to construct the world through story-writing it is necessary for a child no less than for an adult, to become involved in the essence of narrative, to grasp its significance, however tentatively. It is to exercise a critical judgement: to prefer certain words and ideas to others, to feel subject to certain constraints, to define experience in particular ways, to exploit a particular set of opportunities. In short it is to appropriate a form.

Here is how a three-year-old child appropriates narrative form. The author, Elizabeth, dictated her story to a visiting teacher in Vermont USA on a hot, insect infested day in the summer of 1986, accompanying her dictation with pretend writing.

> 'There is a little tea cup in a little tea cup house. There is a little man and a little bug and they flyed and flyed and flyed. He ate some honey. He ate more and more and he got so fat that he had a baby. And that's the end.'

In fifty one measured words Elizabeth captures the very beginning of a practice. First the narrative is set in space, in a timeless present. Next two protagonists are introduced and set off on their adventures. The way is long, the time of action is past. I have suggested that to write a story is to commit yourself to choices. 'They flyed and flyed and flyed' is an early example of just such a choice, dramatising the passage of time in the manner of a formula. In the course of his wanderings the little man commits the story's central act - 'he ate some honey'. He suffers, if that's the right word, the consequences. The story ends.

Elizabeth's story is a schematic outline of the course of many stories, a kind of ideogram - a story of stories. Within the bounds of a three-year-old's experience it is careful and controlled. In an important sense the future course of narrative for Elizabeth will not be capturing new ground but the consolidation of ground already won. Right from the start she knows what it means to be a storyteller.

As with narrative, so with poetry or drama or conversation, and what is true of English is equally true of mathematics or science, history or technology. To learn each subject is to practise an art, where practice implies sustained performance rather than technical exercise. It is like entering a game and finding oneself at once a party to its rules. The clue to intellectual growth, in or out of school, lies in a child's successive performances, week by week and year by year, in the course of a developing practice. This is why meaning is so important. It is not simply that individual performances are meaningful, representing, as they do, a child's various attempts to construct the world. It is rather that the growth of understanding from infancy to old age is best seen as a ceaseless struggle with meaning, a prolonged effort of mind to shape and reshape experience in the face of new evidence, fresh concerns, and developing ideas.

Motivation, from this point of view, lies at the heart of the curriculum. The wishes, fancies, dreams and interests of children cannot be accommodated to a curriculum that has already been determined since they themselves are part of what shapes a curriculum. It has been said, by the Senior Chief HMI, no less, that 'to confuse the description of a curriculum and its design with its delivery is a fatal error.' The error lies rather in the metaphor of delivery itself. It implies that knowledge is a commodity or artefact which can be passed from teacher to pupil, old to young, in a relatively uncomplicated way. But knowledge is not independent of the means by which it is transmitted, as the metaphor of delivery would entice us to suppose. For one thing, knowledge which is not perceived as appropriate to one's own purpose is literally and figuratively useless. It is of no value because it has no application in the individual struggle with meaning. More than this, the transmission of knowledge always implies a challenge to knowledge, as the accumulated wisdom of the past confronts the insistent experience of the present. For all its generosity, *English for Ages 5 to 11* at times forgets this. It speaks for example of 'adding' standard English to non-standard English, or literary language to non-literary language, as if the process were one of simple accretion. But to teach literary language or standard English with any degree of seriousness, granted an appreciation of the meaningfulness of children's thought and action, is to recognise that neither form of language will emerge unscathed from the educational encounter. Thinking seriously about the language of literature with children necessarily alters the literary perception of both pupil and teacher, while any discussion of standard English with a class of, say, eight- or nine year-old children, casts some doubt on the authority or acceptability of the standard itself.

The interdependence of the knowledge which a curriculum transmits and the purposes of the children to whom it is transmitted makes nonsense of the National Curriculum in its present prescriptive form. It is only within the context of classroom life that a curriculum can be appropriately described, let alone effectively implemented. General statements about what is to be learned irrespective of circumstance have little value except as *aides-mémoire*. But let us leave aside, for the time being, this larger issue and ask ourselves how, within the theory of learning outlined above, attainment can best be defined and assessed. For it is in the definition of attainment that the first report of the English Working Group most clearly and most damagingly denies its own best insights.

If the theory which I have sketched is correct, then to follow the course of intellectual development is to chart the history of a critical enterprise. The teacher's responsibility is both to intervene in this enterprise and to interpret it. Intervention is well described in *English for Ages 5 to 11* with its account of the diverse roles which teachers play in the development of young writers, as 'observers, facilitators, modellers, readers and supporters'. But the report has little to say about interpretation, trapped as it is in the ideology of targets and levels of attainment, key stages and standard assessment tasks.

By interpretation I mean the critical scrutiny of children's developing enterprise, moment by moment and phase by phase over the course of children's school lives. The focus of attention is a child's thought and action at its most significant. Our interest is not in simulations of thought, that is to say in exercises, tests, prescribed tasks and periodic examinations, but in the work that is most expressive of each child's struggle with meaning. In the study of English this work includes children's stories and poems, diaries and notebooks, arguments and conversations, play acting and make believe, reflections and speculations on language and literature.

In analysing this body of work the first task is to describe patterns of intention: the interests, motifs, orientations, forms of meditation that govern a child's thought and seek expression in his/her practice. We will want to explore, also, the interplay of form and content in a child's work, subject by subject. One crucial issue concerns the way in which a child's critical enterprise circulates through the various aspects of the curriculum. A nine-year-old's fascination in the borderline between order and disorder, logic and magic, most apparent at first in her storytelling, is seen to extend on closer inspection into her scientific and mathematical investigations. A twelve-year-old's absorption in the life of a frog embraces natural history, art, literature and philosophy with equal enthusiasm. Above all we are concerned with the development of a child's meanings over time - with shifts of focus, apparent impediments, uneven development, the loss and recovery of interest, the endless reinterpretation of ideas, attitudes and achievements.

Whether the national curriculum can be so reconstructed as to place the interpretation of meaning at the centre of assessment and the development of meaning at the centre of attainment is an open question. But from the closing pages of *English for Ages 5 to 11* it is possible to gain some idea of how interpretation would transform the formalistic targets which the working group has bequeathed us. The last of the report's six appendices offers a series of examples of children's work in illustration of 'children's developing writing with reference to our attainment targets'. It is not altogether clear how far the report's commentary on these works is intended to illustrate how written attainments at any given level might best be described, but nothing encourages a reader to suppose that the commentary is other than exemplary. The fourth piece of writing in this series is introduced as 'an unaided first draft by a middle infant girl' (Figure 1).

The report describes this splendid story (Figure 1) in the following way:

'This is a simple chronological account with a clear story structure, including a conventional beginning, narrative middle and end. The sentences are almost all demarcated, though via the graphic, comic-strip layout, and not via capital letters and punctuation. The spelling is almost entirely meaningful and recognisable. In several cases, it shows that the author has correctly grasped the patterns involved, even though the individual spellings are wrong (for example, trooth, eny, owt, sumthing, cubad). The handwriting occasionally mixes upper and lower case letters, though only at beginnings and ends of words, not at random.'

I find it hard to imagine a thinner description of a young child's narrative achievement. At no point in the analysis is there the smallest recognition of the significance of the story, or of the relationship between its meaning and its form, or of the quality of narrative thought which is seeking expression here. A teacher who attempted no more than this by way of description would have little chance of assessing this child's understanding, still less of enhancing it.

Look at the story more closely. Its theme is the moral order and the relationship of that order to experience as perceived by a child of six. It deals with truth

When I was naughty

It wasa ferw weex Past My birthday wen m and My sister went to the Kitchen

I went to the Cybad and Clare opn. the cubad and We tuck the crips and We went up seris My

daP cort me and Cla so he said have you tuck Sum thing from the cubad no we said

then My daD said have you no I lid are you teling lis no no no I lid again In the end My daD mAd me tell the trooth

then he said you naughty gils and sent me and clare to bed with owt eny supa and Clare blamd it on me.

Figure 1 - 'When I was naughty'

and lies, mutuality and recrimination, guilt and blame. Implicitly it addresses the conflict between a child's and an adult's view of these matters which the narrative dramatises and personalises.

After an opening formula - 'It was ... when ... ' - which acts as a rough equivalent of 'Once upon a time ... ' as applied to reminiscence rather than an invention, the first two frames present an uninterrupted flow of action in which words and pictures alike are expressive of spontaneous and uninhibited movement. The tiny canonical sentences hurry by, linked by a series of 'ands', each with its own active verb: 'went', 'opened', 'took', 'went'. The drawings - it would be misleading to call them illustrations - mimic and extend the writing. In the first, one child is already in the kitchen, approaching the cupboard, while the other crosses the living room, with its large round central light. By the second drawing, both children have reached the kitchen and Clare is already opening the cupboard door. The empty living room is still in view, drawing attention to the intervening action. In the third picture, which really accompanies the writing in the second frame, the children are striding upstairs, one of them in the act of stepping from one stair to another.

Up to this point the moral order has not intervened, unless the cupboard carries an implication of guarded space or the words 'we tuck the crips' suggest already the fatefulness of the object of the children's visit to the kitchen! The two children are acting freely in a world in which as yet nothing has been forbidden. Up to this point too, the author's use of personal pronouns suggests the mutuality of the sisters - 'me and my sister went ... I went ... Clare opened ... we tuck ... we went upstairs'. The moral order enters only with the very last word of frame two when the flow of action is brought to an abrupt halt. 'My dad cort me and Clare ... ' The word 'caught' transforms all that has gone before, turning the girls' freedom of action into a transgression, a flouting of the rules. 'My dad *cort* me and Clare', not met, saw, or came across. By the use of this one word the guilt is already acknowledged, an acknowledgement further emphasised in the words that follow - 'so he said ... ' - where the word 'so' implies that the father already suspects or knows the truth. The fourth drawing represents as it were the moment of truth. Dad has appeared in a doorway at the foot of the stairs on which the two sisters are suddenly frozen (notice the feet of the leading sister now).

The confessional scene that follows, frame four, is something of a *tour de force*. The father's successive questions are varied in a manner so exact as to suggest a familiar experience on the part of the six-year-old author, precisely observed and recorded. This is the moment at which mutuality breaks down as the narrator alone acknowledges the deceit. 'No we said ... no I lid ... no no no I lid again.' The rhetoric is decidedly artful. And then, to cut a long story short, 'in the end my dad mad me tell the trooth'. We do not need the how of it. The point is that it is impossible to get away with it. A father's authority, or perhaps it's his trickiness, is sufficient to elicit the truth.

The final frame and its accompanying picture draw out the consequences. The girls are put to bed without any supper. In frame two they seemed controllers of their own destiny - 'we tuck the crips and we went up seris'. Now the tables are turned; 'went' has become 'sent'. The children after all are subject to their father's will. In the final drawing the stairs have grown much deeper. They are no longer the quick, easy passage from kitchen cupboard to children's room. Clare has disappeared, appropriately enough since the adult intervention has destroyed the children's mutuality - 'and Clare blamd it on me'. The narrator, who in acknowledging her guilt has given the game away, is left to face her father's anger alone as he stands at the bottom of the stairs enforcing his order.

'When I was naughty' offers us a vivid glimpse of a young child's narrative thought at its most richly significant. To interpret the story is to begin to understand the achievement of its six-year-old author and to define the quality of her own understanding. Interpretation, in the manner attempted above or something like it, sets the agenda for intervention. It gives us an idea of the books to suggest to the writer as aids to her development. It shows us how to help her address the moral concerns that form the subject of her narrative. It clarifies for us the interplay of text and picture in her narrative enterprise. It helps us to see how to raise with her, however tentatively, the question of narrative voice and narrative identity. It illustrates the significance which she attaches to punctuation and the demarcation of sentences - notice for example the single large full stop, decisively placed at the end of the tale.

The example of this one story demonstrates, it seems to me, the futility of attainment targets as defined by the National Curriculum in its present form. Any means of assessment that lies as it were below the level of interpretation cannot but fail adequately to represent the quality of children's thought. It is the act of interpretation which enables us to recognise whatever is individual or original in a child's achievement, and thus whatever is empowering. By isolating form from meaning, attainment targets reduce intellectual achievement to mere mechanism. At the level of practice such a reductionism encourages teachers not just to ignore but seriously to misconstrue children's meanings. Formal 'weaknesses' are diagnosed irrespective of the critical insights which they serve and which in turn hold the clue to progress. (Look closely at the way in which the six-year-old author of 'When I was naughty' exploits the 'incorrect' or at least non-standard phrase 'me and my sister'. How aptly she turns deficit to advantage.) As for theory, reductionism encourages a false understanding of intellectual growth in which, as I have already argued, significant utterance is perceived as the goal of education rather than its necessary instrument.

The national curriculum rests on a mistake. It is not certain that teachers can correct it but at least we can try. No-one else is in a position to succeed.

Chapter 2

Schools and their governors: building efficient partnerships

Joan Sallis

What can we do that is still legal? This is a question frequently asked by governing bodies in the aftermath of the Education Reform Act. The point is that there are many things we treasure in education which are not actually encouraged by some of the new legislation but which are nevertheless not illegal. We must identify those things together and consider how in the new climate we can hang onto them.

We may not, you see, any longer have the protection of the local education authority, whose role will inevitably change, in maintaining a vision of education as a public service meeting needs rather than a market-place responding to demands. We may have to help ourselves in keeping alive the essential habit of sharing good practice for the benefit of children, rather than allowing the competitive ethic to make us greedy and suspicious, hiding our work like children doing a test. We may have to seek new friends to join us in the preservation of the broad curriculum for all children, not just those whose parents are able to supplement what the school can offer. In this chapter I shall discuss how we can build not just warm and trusting, but also efficient partnerships for the protection of confident teaching and good learning.

The first campaign I was ever involved in was nothing to do with education. It was about children in hospital. I now know that there is a very effective pressure group devoted to their well-being, and it has transformed children's wards in very much the same way as our schools have been transformed over the same twenty odd years. We had moved to a modest house on an estate, where everyone else was new and like us appeared to have three under-fives. One neighbour had been badly treated by our local hospital. Her little boy of two was dying of leukaemia, and she wanted to spend his last days and nights with him. She sat in that ward on a hard chair for seven days and nights and was not offered a bed or a meal or even a cup of tea. She was indeed told many times, not always nicely, to go home and leave the job to the experts.

We became angry and raised some money and we sent it to the hospital asking them to buy a folding bed in the name of our street and that little boy. The money came back with a polite letter saying thank you, but it was not the policy of the hospital to allow parents to stay. So *we* bought the bed and sent it to the hospital.

It was very effective. Our little stone started a slow bureaucratic landslide and the health authority in time built a permanent parent and child unit. The sister in charge of the children's ward was moved after a decent interval to the geriatric ward, where the presence of parents was unlikely to be such a nuisance. Most interesting of all, our action brought to light the fact that the Friends of the Hospital had some time before bought four folding beds for the children's ward, and they were locked in a cupboard and never referred to.

I could have told this story to illustrate how long professionals have taken in health, education, and other fields, to decide that they might be able to do a rather better job with some help from parents, but although that is true, it is not the feature of this experience that has taught me so much and that is so relevant to our present circumstances. I am more interested in the beds in the cupboard. The best structures in the world will not work when human beings do not want them to work, and even quite poor structures work very well if the human beings concerned have common purposes, shared values, and efficient working partnerships. At this dangerous roundabout we have reached, where we could take so many wrong turnings, the greatest danger of all is that because of negative attitudes on the part of teachers, and particularly headteachers, to some of the new structures, we shall miss the chance to find allies for the good fight.

The year 1967 will be remembered for the Plowden Report which set out the stunning message that the greatest single factor in a child's learning progress was the degree of support from home. I did not know that an important government committee was reporting, but I often think now how ironic it was that in that year when we had three children together in the infants, that we never even entered the building, had no open evenings or reports, no communication of any kind. The Plowden Report also started other major changes in train: it taught that learning does not take place in tidy compartments of age and subject, but is a response to an unreturning moment of wonder and curiosity. The changes in primary education which followed responded to both messages, but somehow the development of child-centred methods always raced ahead of the growth of better communication, and parents have never quite kept up with the revolution in the primary classroom - a failure that may cost us dear at this dangerous roundabout.

Most readers will know that I soon became involved in working for better home/school communication in my own town, and that this led to a reform in the antiquated, slightly comic, at best irrelevant and at worst corrupt, system of school government then almost universal. I did not actually believe in participation for its own sake. I believed a wise general practitioner who told me firmly after an unenjoyable birth that his job was to produce live babies, not give me a beautiful experience. It is the same with schools: participation is worth taking a lot of trouble over if it aids learning, but as a means by which people whose lives lack fulfillment might seek to find it, it has nothing to do with education. It has indeed done great damage to the whole concept in many teachers' eyes, and is responsible for those negative feelings of which I spoke.

But in an affluent town where many parents could afford private education, the schools did not have many powerful friends, and it seemed silly to discourage even the non-powerful ones who together might have changed things. All I have ever tried to do is to give non-powerful people confidence that they might have influence as a group, and to persuade professionals to share their responsibilities with such people and even help them organise.

In September 1974, we started a system of school governors based on equal representation of all groups and sharing all decisions at school level. It came as a result of public pressure, but I believe our council at the time thought it was only a charade, so it did not matter who wore the funny hats. On that date there were only five local education authorities out of 104 who had given up their own control of school governors. On 31 August 1988 there were still only five, but on 1 September 1988 there were 104. That is a measure of the revolution we have lived through, so no wonder we feel stunned.

Because the pilot reform in our small town transformed the outlook for state education, I was asked to represent parents on the Taylor Committee, which reported in 1977 on the whole question of school governors, and indeed on the wider question of how schools made their decisions and communicated with their public. That Committee recommended that all schools should have their own governors; that they should represent an equal partnership of all interests; that they should share in all school-level decisions; that they should be responsible for good communication and relationships; that they should work openly; and that they should be trained. Because of opposition from the teacher unions the Labour Government which had set up the Committee and to which it reported could not legislate on these proposals, though it would have been ready to do so. We had to wait ten years for our partnership because of negative attitudes on the part of teachers. In my view they totally miscalculated the prospects for state education in a contracting service, and assumed too readily that the well resourced system we had had and the teacher's freedom within it would last for ever. I hope they will not make the same mistakes again, because we have another chance - in vastly less favourable circumstances - to build some powerful alliances for schools.

I spoke of dangerous turnings we might take. I have already referred to the possibility that schools will be driven to compete instead of cooperating, and that instead of trying to make good practice grow for all children they will bury their own in the ground like the talents in the parable.

I have also referred to the lack of adequate public understanding of primary school methods, and the danger here is that primary schools will lose confidence in what they have been doing over twenty years, which to me has been like an old sepia photograph bursting into colour. They need not lose confidence, because HMI have produced plenty of evidence (especially in the 1978 Survey) that schools which concentrate heavily on basics do not in fact do as well in basics as those offering a richer curriculum. But do parents know this? Do they know that drawing round your feet has anything to do with area, that sailing corks and weighing rice is maths and science, that visits to the churchyard have lessons in subtraction as well as social and local history? If primary teachers are afraid to stray from the paths that lead to standard assessment tests, they may forget that it is beyond the paths that the flowers grow. Tragic, since many children only ever go on a voyage of discovery with the school, and narrowing the curriculum will once more damage most seriously those whose lives have few open windows. Yet parents' understandable anxiety will bring about such a sad outcome if we cannot rapidly improve communication about how classroom activity fits into rigorous learning plans.

I also worry about the fashionable word 'relevance'. Yes, of course we must not forget that if we do not earn a good living as a nation, we cannot afford good schools or hospitals, subsidies to the arts and improvements in the environment. But one is bound to notice that relevance is preached by some very powerful and influential people who have reached those positions of power and influence through the great privilege of an irrelevant education, and are choosing it for their children. Why so earnestly advocate something different for the rest of us? Also relevance is a concept handed down from one stage of education to another. We need to do well in the infants, so we can do well in the juniors, flourish in the secondary school, to meet the needs of higher education and employment. Is it not like a pair of shoes handed down in a large poor family, fitting worse and looking worse with each new owner? Primary schools have a right to their own goals as children have a right to their own shoes, and if that means responding to that unreturning moment I spoke of, so be it.

Finally, I am anxious lest the power intended to be transferred from local education authorities to parents and governors finds its way into the wrong hands. It could find its way to headteachers. I would not think that healthy. It could revert to central government. It could be seized by extremist minority groups of various kinds, and I know schools fear this. The only defence, in education as in politics, against too much power at the centre, or too much power with extremists, is participation by a large number of ordinary people.

Negative attitudes to the new structures of participation could expose us all to these dangers, since these could make teachers pay too little attention to sharing values, justifying methods, and promoting wide participation.

Now I come to the current legislation, the structures, good and not so good, especially those on schools and governors. My impression is that there is a great deal of confusion now about the Education Acts of 1986 and 1988, what provisions are in which Act, which of the former remain in force, if any, and which have been overtaken by the subsequent legislation. Not only heads and teachers suffer from this: more than one Director of Education has asked me to speak to heads about the Education Reform Act and looked quite bewildered at my suggestion that I might also cover the very important provisions of the 1986 Act. This is natural, when so much has been thrown at us so fast, but it is also very dangerous. Most people in the education service have negative attitudes in some degree towards the Education Reform Act. They see it as undermining local government, reducing the independence of teachers, threatening the full, free and fair provision for children, and setting school against school in cut-throat competition. I would accept that analysis and share those fears. Yet if professionals extend such perceptions to the 1986 Act they will be locking in cupboards the very structures that can help them implement the later legislation with proper regard for those values I spoke of - sharing good practice, meeting needs, preserving the full curriculum, promoting wide participation, and communicating well with their public.

The 1986 Act has the support of all political parties. It is broadly speaking still the law of the land. It is no more likely to go away than trial by jury. It is not about undermining local government, devaluing teachers, forcing schools to compete, or threatening the full, free and fair education we value. It is only about how schools make their decisions. It gives schools the means to build partnerships of caring and wise people who will have great power and who may, properly supported and informed, trusted and valued, use that power well for children.

Teachers and headteachers have considerable scope for influencing the development and use of these structures if they have positive attitudes to them, attitudes free from fear, patronage, or territorialism. They need to keep separate in their minds the movement towards greater involvement of governors and parents on the one hand and the pressure towards a market-driven service on the other. Both trends exist and both are strong, but they are not necessarily connected, and they could well pull in different directions if professionals want it that way. But professionals need to familiarise themselves with the provisions of the 1986 Act and determine to make it work well in their schools. Its main features are the creation of governing bodies balanced in composition, sharing decisions about school life, working openly, communicating with parents and the wider community, and within themselves affording equal rights to all groups. If these principles are not honoured in the way schools operate the rules, we shall have our market-driven service with a vengeance, and run the risk that the power which no longer rests with the local education authority will find its way either into the hands of central government or those of unrepresentative and possibly self-seeking minorities. The defensive teacher has always been the worst enemy of a well-resourced and well-respected service, since these things require public pressure, and public pressure will only come from a sense of ownership of that service. Territorialism will now also be the enemy of a full curriculum, a sharing cooperative service, a service meeting needs.

If schools care enough about involving the right people in the new structures, they will work even harder to achieve broadly based participation in those structures. They will in every way encourage ordinary people to accept responsibility, telling them that it is their ordinariness which is wanted. They will make sure that participation is real, not a game, because cynicism on that score is one of the greatest deterrents to participation. They will explain their policies in simple jargon-free language, seeking consent and support. They will communicate the respect they have for parents from all backgrounds and their high expectations of them and their children. They will make parents feel, not just welcome, but *needed*.

As for governors, headteachers must shed their bad associations with a discredited old system and make up their minds that things will be different from now on. The biggest problem is that heads see governors as external to the school, thrown at it from a distance like a custard pie, but not half so funny. They whinge to each other at their conferences about governors if they are awful, and congratulate themselves mildly if they are not too bad. They did not after all choose them, so why should they accept any responsibility for the quality of their work? They did not choose the teachers they inherited when they were appointed either, yet they accept that good management includes identifying and orchestrating the talents of the team, negotiating objectives, creating a climate of high expectation and commitment, building structures to ensure smooth harmonious working together, and meeting the development needs of individuals. Only when heads accept similar responsibility for the quality of governors' work, and regard it as a test of their own leadership skills, shall we advance.

The relationship with governors must be open, sharing, willing. High expectations must be conveyed - they will improve the good governor and squeeze out in time the hopelessly unsuitable one. Structures must be created to enable governors to become familiar with the school, get beyond the carol service and harvest festival level of involvement. They cannot just 'drop in' but need a framework, a purpose, a regular responsibility. Duty governor of the month, governor taking a special interest in one aspect of school life, governor adopting a class, governor shadowing a teacher, anything which brings confidence and real contact. Once heads are proud of the extent to which they share, afford access, give information, build efficient working relationships, genuinely seek the new perspectives of outsiders on school problems, because that is part of good management, governors will improve.

Schools must also work to share their thinking with governors and parents, not feel that they have to be a step ahead because they are professionals. In a situation where change comes so fast and all the service has indigestion, a huge obstacle to progress is the professionals' feeling that they must possess understanding themselves before they can share, keep a step ahead, have the answer book. Headteachers especially must ensure that the business and procedures of school government really are such as to promote an active role for all governors, and this means eschewing special exclusive relationships, protecting the weak and making space for them, insisting that all the rules about openness and equality of all governors are observed, being relaxed about governors doing their own communication with parents and community. There will be misunderstanding and the occasional clumsiness, but are these not trivial compared with the dangers a good partnership could help us avoid?

Can we do it? In bad moments I doubt it, because I see everywhere such a lot of retreat into even more territorial habits, as power to the parents and governors gets all mixed up in people's minds with the fear of the market-place philosophy and all the destructive things it could do to schools. Yet I so clearly see the scope for sharing with parents and governors all the good things that go on in schools, winning their hearts and minds for the battle to preserve those things, and on good days hope the schools will soon see it that way too. The stakes are high, and the time we have is very short.

Chapter 3

How to achieve effective learning in spite of the Education Reform Act

Brian Simon

Curriculum, and learning, operate within a specific context, and that context determines in a direct way the nature and direction of the learning processes. In looking at how to achieve effective learning in spite of the Education Reform Act, I will focus on context, on structure, because we need to be aware both of the threats and dangers, and of the possibilities existing in the post-ERA situation. It is important to analyse the situation in order to assess the effects of the different scenarios now fighting for hegemony - for the promotion of effective learning in our schools.

The Education Reform Act is certainly primarily an attack on local government and its control, through democratic procedures of local school systems. Local government, of course, has suffered and is suffering many other attacks in terms of the deliberate undermining of its financial viability and scope for action - the attack on the educational front is only part of this, if a key aspect. The clear aim of all this is to downgrade local authorities, and so that form of local democracy which certainly has a long historical tradition in this country. The favoured method is to release parent power as a counterweight. The clear aim is, by 'freeing' schools from local authority control, to establish a free market in schooling. This thrust is fuelled by the ideology of competition (as brilliantly analysed by Ted Wragg, (1988)). The expectation is that good schools will drive out bad (in contradistinction to Gresham's law).

This then is the desired scenario; schools, increasingly independent (sometimes altogether independent) of local authorities competing with each other for 'customers' - otherwise they go down the drain. Schools are to be judged against each other in terms of test results.

This form of competition, it is expected, will penetrate deeply into the life of every school. That is what I mean by the context, by which the educational processes of the future will be determined - or at the least affected. The issue then becomes - how do we promote effective learning in conditions of severe competition of school against school?

What will be the effect of this on children's learning within the individual school - primary and secondary? That is the sort of issue we need to examine. That is, at least, the hoped for outcome of those supporting this measure. Those who view such an outcome with distaste need to consider how to develop an alternative scenario, where truly educational values predominate. I will come back to this in due course.

One major objective of the Education Reform Act, although nowhere stated, is to destroy our existing system of comprehensive primary and secondary schools. After many battles, lasting at least thirty years, and much endeavour, that system is on the edge of reaching fruition; its rewards were just becoming apparent, and I say this advisedly in spite of the years of media and political/industrial attacks on these schools, much of it prejudiced and ill-informed. The direct assault on this system, as at Solihull a few years ago, failed dismally, as we all know, being totally rejected by the local population in spite of a favourable (local) political situation. But the powers that be were determined to make a change. The political situation seemed ripe. The strategy chosen is circumvention. The tactics, the establishment of a new category of opted out, or grant-maintained schools, under no form of local democratic control, and the foundation of a new category of school alongside those now existing - the city technology colleges.

This, we should realise, is conceived as a long-term strategy. Margaret Thatcher announced it clearly: 'You are going to have three systems,' she said, shortly after the last election, 'first there will be those who wish to stay with the local authorities . . . [then] you are going to have direct grant schools [by which she meant schools directly funded by the state] . . . and then you are going to have a private sector with assisted places.' 'That,' she added, 'is variety.' It would give 'wider choice of public provision' for 'people who are not satisfied'.

We should not underestimate the government's determination to bring this about. Indeed, on this aspect of the Act (and this is its central thrust without a doubt) the government has shown a steely purpose. Even before the Bill received Royal Assent, the Grant Maintained School Trust, headed by a Conservative MP, was established. To make a striking success of the opting-out sections of the Act is a political imperative for the present government. Reputations - and futures - depend on it. It is well known that the Prime Minister hopes all, or the great majority of schools, will in fact opt out. This then is one arena where battle lines are drawn. What is the situation?

First, the great bulk of the first forty or fifty schools considering opting out are in fact schools that are escaping local government reorganisation plans. The bulk of those schools considering opting out have in fact been what Judith Judd, of the *Observer*, describes as 'lame ducks' - schools mostly faced with closure, amalgamation, or some such change. The first two to vote to take this option were Skegness Grammar and Audenshawe High, one from a Tory, one from a Labour authority. The former Secretary of State made the most of these first 'successes' for the new policy. 'These two schools,' he said, 'have been bold enough to grasp the opportunity to control their own destinies. They have been quick to see the advantages of their new freedom . . . . They will be an example for others to follow.' (*Times Educational Supplement*, 1989).

But what else do we note about this campaign? Two aspects are of interest. First, comprehensive schools in affluent, suburban areas, which were originally expected to seize this option, are in fact so far conspicuous by their absence - a point well worth noting. Second, there has been no rush to opt out from the so-called 'loony left' councils at all, as yet. I will not list them, since the description is probably libellous at present. Far from there having been a rush to opt out by these schools, what has emerged is an apparently high degree of loyalty to the relevant local authorities. The issue is far from satisfactory in terms of the future scenario desired by the Government which I depicted above.

But we cannot only observe the situation - we need to act. A strong defensive structure is being built up round school systems locally. The Association of Municipal Authorities, quite legitimately, has made very clear its total opposition to opting out, with the publication of a first class booklet giving guidance on the issue. Not only Labour but also Conservative authorities are campaigning against opting out. Conservative authorities can be as proud of their local systems as those of other political persuasions. The Tory shire counties generally also oppose this measure. It may be that the Government has misjudged the feel or mood of the country, perhaps too strongly influenced by London conditions and experience.

There is clearly an underestimation of the level of support for local comprehensive systems in areas like the Midlands (Leicestershire for instance); and especially in areas like Lancashire and Yorkshire. Many of these authorities are proud of their systems, and determined to maintain and develop them for the future. The local authorities themselves are becoming more flexible, are evolving more effective forms of partnership with parents and governors, becoming less bureaucratic - to use the modern jargon, more customer-friendly. I conclude that local authorities should be encouraged to take the lead in defence of their systems - that they should not kowtow to any bullying by those in authority on this matter. But to do this effectively they need support from teachers and their organisations, from the Labour movement, from governors and their organisations, and from community organisations of all types, including churches. Out of this form of active cooperation could come new structures, holding a hope for the future - and incidentally affecting positively the feel, ethos and morale of individual schools - conditions surely required for effective learning within them.

My conclusion is that on this crucial issue honours so far are about even. The future depends on changes in the balance of forces. What is needed is clear leadership, and then specific and decisive action, on both a local and national level. Our aim must be to retain control of our schools for ourselves and for the whole of the local community - and energetically to resist the attempt to set individual groups of parents within that community at loggerheads, competing against each other and so, finally, destroying each other. This is what the government seems to want, and what will happen unless we prevent it, as I am sure we can.

If things have not gone the government's way with opting out, nor have they in relation to city technology colleges (CTCs). Whatever may be the arguments for this initiative, one thing is certain - their presence will disrupt local systems of comprehensive education. But the twenty CTCs promised by Mr Baker to the Conservative party conference in October 1987 (for which he received a standing ovation) have been reduced to five or six as a maximum by the early 1990s, although an upper limit of twenty has apparently been set by the Treasury. Also it is well known that industry, in general, has clearly distanced itself from involvement. Vast sums of taxpayers' money are now being siphoned into this scheme. In Nottingham, for instance, £8 million of our money is going to the establishment of one such college, situated in an area already well served by local comprehensives. This is four times the total capital allocation to Nottinghamshire as a whole. Is this a reasonable use of public resources?

Overall hangs the threat of the voucher system as the next stage; indeed this is again being actively argued - by Stuart Sexton and others. Local management of schools is to come in on a formula basis, related to pupil numbers. This might ease the way for the substitution of vouchers for funding from the state (even if that money is taken from the local authorities). So the way might be clear for the transformation of the whole system to one which its supporters describe as 'state independent schools' - a problematic phrase, as a moment's thought makes clear. At the same time the campaign against local authorities continues, with the publication of pamphlets like Sheila Lawler's 'Away with LEAs'.

We need to launch a counterattack against all this. Such a measure - the introduction of vouchers as proposed, together with open entry and the rest, would inevitably transform our system into one closely reflecting the various levels in our social hierarchy. If this came about, our system really would exemplify the French sociologist Bourdieu's image of a school system constructed to ensure exact reproduction of existing social relations. This, of course, is politically a thoroughly conservative objective. It was Anne Sofer who originally pointed out that the opting out proposals in the Bill in fact embodied a profoundly conservative objective - that of preserving the status quo. She writes:

'The most basic and primitive motive any group of people ... has for acting collectively is in self-defence .... The one thing that can be guaranteed to start up the whole campaigning rigmarole is a perceived threat to the status quo. Grammar schools, for which comprehensive reorganisation is planned, schools facing a tertiary college reorganisation, any school with falling rolls threatened with amalgamation, all of these will be able to mobilise effectively to make a bid to opt out. Already most of the schools that are quoted in the press as talking about the possibility fall into this category.'

This was written in July 1987, when the consultation paper on grant maintained schools first appeared. Events have proved her right. So much for the vaunted 'radicalism' of the main feature of the Education Reform Act.

I have spent considerable time on the structural aspects. But this is one area where the battles for the future are being fought, and where they will continue to be fought over the months and years to come. How can I link this to the central issue - of the promotion of effective learning in our schools? This, after all, is not so difficult - the relations are direct.

CONDITIONS FOR EFFECTIVE LEARNING

Some of the essential conditions which I think all, or most, would agree are conducive to effective learning can be defined. First by a long way I would put the morale of the teachers, and of all those involved in schools and schooling. This is a complex issue, but none would deny that over the last few years teachers have been subjected to multiple pressures which show no signs of abating; their negotiating rights have been summarily removed, and no-one knows if and when these will be restored. Teachers' organisations have been denied any part in promoting the new structures and objectives now being imposed - in sharp contradiction to what was the case prior to the passage of the 1944 Act. The imposition of a National Curriculum from above, again without any effective form of consultation, was intended to downgrade, and has downgraded the public's perception of the professional expertise of the teaching profession. There has been only minimal involvement by selected teachers on the subject working parties, as also on the curriculum and assessment councils. The result is a fairly massive alienation of the teaching profession as a whole. A main condition, then, for the promotion of learning must be a deliberate policy, comprising a series of measures, aimed at overcoming this alienation which has now reached a stage where leading teachers and others are advising young people not, under any circumstance, to enter the profession - given existing conditions of service. This involves not only paying teachers properly, and ensuring proper conditions of work - above all allowing time for both primary and secondary teachers during the school day for preparation, marking, reflection and discussion, but also finding the means by which teachers can enter once again into the mainstream of educational policy formation and decision-making. It also involves official, and other, public appreciation for the work of teachers in contradistinction from the situation that has developed over the last ten or fifteen years - that of holding the teachers responsible for all the ills of society. Many of you will remember Sir Arnold Weinstock's comment in the mid-1970s, shortly after the oil price rise: 'I blame the teachers'. It is, perhaps ironic that the very same Weinstock has recently been under more or less continuous criticism in the financial pages of the quality press for his mismanagement and especially for his own financial failures as head of one of Britain's greatest industrial complexes, GEC. It really is too easy to 'blame the teachers'.

Second, perhaps oddly, I would put as an important condition for the promotion of effective learning an atmosphere of stability - hastening to add that by that I do not mean stagnation. But stability is needed so that all concerned can concentrate on the job in hand, and do not have to spend time and energy looking over their shoulders much of the time to assess where the next threat is coming from. That is why the existing pressures from government aimed directly at destabilising local authorities is so inimical to what one might call good practice in the schools. Destabilised local authorities mean destabilised schools. While a few authorities, mostly around London, may have given some reason for their characterisation as 'loony left' (or 'loony right' for that matter), generally speaking the mass of the 100-odd authorities in this country are carrying out their functions, in spite of increasingly difficult conditions, in an exemplary manner - and this includes their main responsibility - education. The fight against opting out and against CTCs is also a fight for stability - for the preservation of the most positive aspects of present structures and systems. Stability also provides the conditions for evolution, and so for planned and considered change. A major task for the next ten years, many think, and one of increasing urgency, is the development of an effective system of tertiary education for the sixteen- to eighteen-year-olds which would give direction and purpose to the compulsory years up to sixteen. Such tertiary systems must build on existing comprehensive systems and relate directly to them. They must also be uncompromisingly comprehensive. Without this initiative, Britain will fall still further behind comparable countries. We are already far at the bottom of the league in the proportion of the sixteen- to eighteen-year-olds still in full-time education and training. This is a major, urgent and immediate issue. This is where the thrust for the future should be made rather than focusing on breaking up local systems and promoting internecine battles wherever possible. Such a project is progressive, radical if you like, - even modernising. It is certainly educationally necessary and overdue. Its effective implementation requires a stable base in the school system generally.

Third, I would stress the need for cooperation, rather than competition, as the watchword for the future. This government places its faith in competition as the main motivator within and between schools - all must compete against each other, and at all levels. That this will improve standards is no more than an act of faith. In any competitive system, some come out on top and some come out bottom. Probably the degree of success could be equated, by statisticians, to our old friend the normal distribution curve. If this is so there can be no guarantee that the general move is upwards. It might just as well be downwards. A better recipe for overall success, I suggest, is cooperation, or the solidarity engendered in a mutual endeavour. I believe that a good model for this might be Stewart Mason's Leicestershire during the 1960s when a deliberate attempt was made, in all sorts of complex ways, at raising awareness or consciousness; where the stress was put on the value of participation in a common enterprise, having clear objectives. Other authorities I am sure could be cited here. But in a situation where all assist all, where there is agreement as to objectives, where no-one directly benefits from the shortcomings or discomfiture of others - there you have a situation for genuinely mutual cooperation, for the exchange of experience, for free learning one from the other, and the lift of involvement in a common venture. Is it impossible even to consider such a scenario for the future? I believe not. Indeed I believe that to create just such an ethos is a necessity - both locally and nationally.

Finally it is important, I suggest, that there should be, and be seen to be, fair and equal allocation of resources to all engaged in the enterprise. This is an important principle, though clearly not popular with the powers that be. It is a principle on which local authorities have determined their policies in the past, and at present, accepting that such an authority has a responsibility for the provision of education *equally for all* - and the emphasis is on the words 'for all'. And this is the material basis for turning education into a cooperative enterprise. It may be that there could be *principled* exceptions to this, and I mean principled; exceptions that can be defined and argued on rational grounds, and come to achieve general acceptance. An example might be a policy of positive discrimination, as advocated by Plowden and implemented to some extent in the education priority areas, by which a higher than average proportion of available public resources are allocated to particular groups of children, in this case defined as deprived, or disadvantaged. This could clearly be an exception to the principle of equal provision of resources. Before comprehensive reorganisation there used to be a generally accepted rational justification for the provision of greater resources to another specific group - those selected for grammar or technical schools. This found its rationale in the theory and practice of intelligence testing - that is, in arguments as to the supposed inborn, fixed and unchangeable nature of the child, and of differences between children, which were held to be largely genetically determined and also accurately measurable. It was partly because this particular theory or ideology gained so strong a hold in this country 30 or 40 years ago that the move to comprehensive education was delayed here compared to what happened, for instance, in Sweden or Japan. But at least the issue was open to rational argument. When this ideology collapsed - and so failed to receive public support - the way was open to comprehensive education, and so to the *equal* provision of resources (which must be scarce) to all. But in fact this concept - that of the equal provision of education as a public good - was written into the 1944 Act, with its perspective of secondary education for all. On what other principle could the public provision of education find its justification, particularly in time of war, when equal sacrifices were demanded from all, and as freely given?

The market-place philosophy cannot of course lead to equality of provision and does not seek to. That is another reason why those espousing it seek to loosen the malign grip, as they see it, of local authorities over their systems of schools. I suggest that the rejection of this philosophy, as a main motive force for change, is essential if we want to create appropriate conditions, or establish an appropriate context, which will act to support and reinforce the endeavour of the schools and teachers to maximise effective learning into the 1990s.

So we come to what is, of course, the greatest issue of all - the actual process of teaching and learning that goes on, day in and day out, in the schools themselves. To some, the matter is unproblematic. And this goes, I am afraid, for the perpetrators of the Education Reform Act. Parliament is now responsible directly for the curriculum. Ministers of State make pronouncements - but they also actually directly determine the curriculum itself, and of course also the means, forms and nature of assessment, which is also now a statutory matter. So, how do these politicians (and I am *not* against politicians, let me make clear) think about, conceptualise if you like, the process of teaching and learning? To take almost at random one example from a DES press release

> 'Confidence and competence are essential qualities for teachers,' says Angela Rumbold. 'New teachers must be properly prepared to deliver the National Curriculum' Education Minister Angela Rumbold said today in a lecture on Initial Training for the future. 'Following the National Curriculum, Initial Training is the next step towards raising standards in schools.' 'Teachers,' she went on 'will need to be confident in their subject knowledge. If they are not, they will not be able to stretch their pupils. We need to be sure that teachers will be able to transmit their knowledge effectively to allow pupils the joys of learning rather than the drudge of sitting in a classroom.'

Now I know this is only a press release - even if the lecture was delivered at the Cambridge Institute of Education - though it does quote her actual words. Perhaps it is unfair to examine the precise use of language too closely. Nevertheless the words chosen are symptomatic of the managerial, essentially philistine, top-down approach which now prevails in these circles. The whole concept of 'delivering' the curriculum, as if it were a package of fish and chips, is and must be antipathetic for most teachers or educationalists. It embodies a certain very specific conception as to what education is all about. Now take the final sentence: 'we need to be sure that teachers will be able to transmit their knowledge effectively to allow pupils the joys of learning rather than the drudge of sitting in a classroom'. Of course most pupils would enjoy an entertaining performance. But the 'joy of learning', as such only comes basically when you do your learning for yourself - make it your own. To do this you need abilities and skills. Teaching is hardly a matter of 'transmitting' knowledge - effectively or not. No-one can 'transmit' an ability; nor for that matter is any child born with any given abilities or skills. They may, perhaps, be born with a predisposition towards the mastery of certain abilities - musical or mathematical, for instance. But the actual ability itself is and must be formed through a complex process of activity - both physical and mental - the two often closely related to each other. The teacher oversees, guides, provides for, encourages that activity, according to her understanding as to what forms are appropriate. Education - the promotion of learning - in short, is in no sense a simple process that can be encapsulated in words like those chosen by Angela Rumbold - it is highly complex. Its reduction to a simplistic, crude terminology - and to a parallel level of language - down-grades the real job of the teacher and educator, and undervalues the process, legitimises the introduction of undertrained so-called licensed teachers and others, and does no-one a service.

I conclude that, in the new dispensation now with us, bodies such as the Curriculum Association have an essential function - both to educate our masters (and mistresses) as to the real nature of education as a process, and to grasp back from the politicians the central area of teaching and learning in the schools. This is a task of overriding importance.

References

Times Educational Supplement, (1987), 2 October

Times Educational Supplement, (1989), 24 February

Wragg, T., (1988), *Education in the Market Place*, NUT, London

Chapter 4

The present state of education and its future prospects

Tim Brighouse

CHANGING EDUCATIONAL VALUES

In this chapter I shall discuss changing educational values that particularly concern me. But, before I do, let me just note that when I went into Oxfordshire, in 1978, the debate was all about accountability and falling rolls. In 1976, James Callaghan launched the Great Debate and we all talked of the pending problem of falling rolls.

The next two points are current concerns and I think it is very important that we note the difference. They are to do with market forces, and autonomy. I would balance autonomy against accountability. Much of the current debate is about accountability but I think that is more apparent than real. Actually I think we are into a debate about increased autonomy of institutions and we are relying on market forces in order to secure some sort of healthy state. Looking at the legislation, the words 'choice' and 'competition' keep cropping up. *Choice*, parental choice, is one of the main thrusts of the Education Reform Act of 1988. *Competition*: all the talk is of the worst sort of competition - the simple, easy competition between people and institutions. What is being set up is as unequal a state of public competition as if I were to face Carl Lewis in a 100 metre dash. It is not about the best form of competition which is competition against yourself and against your own previous performance.

Market forces are behind open enrolment, local management of schools and opting out. But what is the market index? For me, the market index is undoubtedly going to be making a market out of children. I have become quite depressed recently at the thought of the conversations in ten years' time that parents will have about their children's progress - and about how those children will be described. Unless we are very careful, we may construct a really awful system of assessment. Once you have assessment you have created a market index by which parental choice can be exercised in order to find out what is the comparative position of schools. You are then in a position where professionals may begin to say, 'It would be a good idea to measure children when they come to us so that we can know whether we are being blamed fairly.' There does seem to be that kind of mood within the profession at the moment. I heard it in one authority recently where an inspector, talking to a group of teachers, said, 'Don't worry. When the parents come in and complain, providing we've got this national system, it won't be just your word. You will have the decision of a big, nationally validated system behind you that says the kid really is level two - even if she or he is nine or ten years old.'

What I am bothered about is not actually whether we are 'fireproof' professionally, but what the impact of all this will be on children as they go through the schooling system. As far as second chance education is concerned, there is quite a good prospect of generating the need for plenty of second chances!

There is also the pecking order by institution, which becomes an extended one:

Institutional hierarchy

Independent major

Independent minor

City technology colleges

Grammar school

Grant-aided/maintained (opted out)

Church aided

Rural county

Urban metro

What this table shows is a longer pecking order of schools than there used to be - and we can predict the outcome of that - a shortage of teachers, already with us. Also we will certainly have both some excellent schools - and some appalling schools. There will not really be a system at all, because there is no intention of having a system; a market is being created. So, we have a contrast which boils down to the emphasis of competition between people as opposed to competition against yourself.

The other image is 'exclusive' rather than 'inclusive'. The whole thrust of comprehensive education is a bold attempt towards inclusiveness rather than exclusiveness; towards enabling people to benefit and to grow up towards confident, and competent, autonomous adulthood - which should be the aim of all educators wherever we are in the system. Think back to the teachers who made a difference to you as children, or think of them today: the most successful practitioners, whether in adult work, community work, or in schools, are those who give the feeling, a genuine feeling, that everybody can enter into this rather exciting world that we are about to explore together. There is no sense of 'It's OK for you and me. The rest of you get on with something else for a while.' The system should be inclusive rather than exclusive; that is what we are working towards.

For me, the purpose of education is summarised brilliantly by the writings of Temple, an archbishop who put even the Bishop of Durham in the shade.

Temple talked about education being the difference between potential and actual worth. (We have to ignore the male terminology as this was written in 1942):

> 'Until education does far more work than it has had an opportunity of doing, you cannot have society organised on the basis of justice. For this reason there will always be a strain between what is due to a man in view of his humanity, with all his powers and capabilities, and what is due to him at the moment, as a member of society, with all his faculties still undeveloped, with many of his tastes warped, with his powers largely crushed. Are you going to treat people as what they might become, or as what they are? Morality requires, I think, that you should treat a person as what he might become, as what he has it in him to become. Business, on the other hand, requires that you should treat him as what he is.'

Actually that image of what 'is' and what 'might be' runs right through education. What I object to in the current legislation is that it is going to use people who are not yet adult, and their progress, as the only market index we have got in order to judge the effectiveness of the schooling system. 'You cannot get rid of the strain except by raising what he is to the level of what he might become. That is the whole work of education ... '

We are in that business every day, particularly of working with people who have not developed their potential.

> 'Give a person the full development of his powers and there will no longer be that conflict between the claim of the man 'as he is' and the claim of the man 'as he might become'. You can have no justice at the basis of your social life until education has done its full work. You can have no real freedom because, until a man's whole personality has been developed, he cannot be free in his own life. And you cannot have political freedom, any more than you can have moral freedom, until people's powers are developed.'

One of our abiding problems in this country is that we regard democracy as a 'uniquely British given idea' as opposed to a principle and a continuum towards which we are moving (or from which we are moving away). We cannot get it, we are nowhere near it, until we have done more work in education than we have done in the past because we have not given that autonomy to sufficient numbers of adults. 'Again, you cannot have political freedom any more than moral freedom until people's powers are developed, for the simple reason that over and over again we find people with a cause which is just who cannot argue it in a way which will enable it to prevail.'

This is a true story from the time of the miners' strike. It is about two young people in London, both nineteen years old, one from Oxfordshire - whom I knew well - and one from Doncaster who had opted out of the school system from the age of fourteen. Standing beside each other in a demonstration, they were knocked to the ground and subsequently carried away. Charges were brought against them and they were brought before a magistrate. Guess which one got the prison sentence and which one got off? The Oxfordshire youth, of course. Now that is not a story against the police or the justice system. It is a story against a society that has not yet taken the business of raising everybody to the amazing potential that I believe is there because we are fettered by a system - and have been in the past - that requires a vast number of people to fail. Temple gave this lovely image: 'There exists a mental form of slavery which is as real as any economic form. We are pledged to destroy it and if you want human liberty you must have educated people.' In R. A. Butler's memoirs that philosophy informed the pioneers of the time. Butler was bothered that a half per cent in private education had risen to two per cent before the war. They were worried by Temple's words: 'You cannot have political freedom, you cannot have social justice, so long as people can buy a better chance in life.' Nowadays we have retreated a long way from those ideals - and they are ideals that, for me, matter a lot, leading as they do towards inclusive rather than exclusive systems of education.

Next I want to explore the ways in which it may be possible to frustrate notions of harmful competition and encourage notions of interdependence ... that will provide shining examples of the sort of practice of use when the 1988 Education Reform Act is replaced, as I am sure it must be, by a new Act at the end of the century. There is no question that it *will* be replaced - it is only a question of when there will be a swing in the other direction towards a concern for social justice, for looking after the development of everybody. Historically, such a swing is inevitable. The Government is seriously destabilising the system, which I do not think it realises.

THE PROCESS OF CHANGE

Anyone who has been in the game of change will probably be familiar with the four stages of the process of change:

Stage 1	Unconscious incompetence
Stage 2	Conscious incompetence
Stage 3	Conscious competence
Stage 4	Unconscious competence

Of course, you do not change everything all at once. You change bits of things so that people can move from incompetence to competence quickly. But the Government is not doing this, and that is why there is a shortage of teachers because they are all thinking, 'it would be a better thing to do something else, anything else, rather than be a teacher and have to cope with all this incredible change'.

What you have to do is get the pace right, orchestrate it, and you can move on. But just look at what teachers - headteachers especially - are currently having to deal with in the way of change:

- New governors
- Sex education
- Political bias
- Suspension
- TVEI
- Low attainers
- GCSE
- National Curriculum
- Religious education (RE)
- Charging
- Complaints
- Local management of schools (LMS)
- GRIST
- Records of achievement
- Staff appraisal
- Draft orders on the curriculum

Things are seriously destabilised. It is difficult to sort out the urgent from the important. But if you want to get people out of being unconsciously incompetent you want to lift them, raise their morale. So what happens? You have got to hand it to the Government: what managers would start off by threatening the dire consequences of what will happen to you if there are complaints against you while you are implementing all this change?

STRATEGIES

My advice would be to get involved in it as little as possible. A sense of priority is vital, and number one is the priority of going back to those principles I mentioned above. You have to try and enable more children, more people in the community, to unlock their talent.

As teachers, the goal in the next five to ten years, as the system collapses as a system, is to produce exemplars of what works as opposed to what does not work. It can be done in the classroom, by all sorts of small decisions about how to present children's performance to parents and public and in many other organisational decisions both within individual schools and among several schools.

LOCAL FINANCIAL MANAGEMENT OF SCHOOLS (LMS)

Local management of schools (LMS) is an important area, and unfortunately local education authorities are about to walk into a real problem. One big issue that will drive schools to become grant-maintained against their better judgment is the financial information systems that they are going to be given.

I think local education authorities have got to think very seriously indeed if they do not want schools to become grant-maintained due to financial systems - and because hundreds of teachers, headteachers and governors are wound up into fury by hopeless information. After all if a school becomes grant-maintained it is going to receive money direct by monthly instalments. I think that there is a lot of mileage in giving schools control of all except salaries and finding a way to make sure that there is real commitment - accounting by the schools that go into local financial management. Local education authorities would not like them to opt out for the wrong reason.

Another point is the allocation of the general schools budget. There are mandatory exceptions, the seven or ten per cent discretionary items, and there are the staff involved in schools. Most people in the system, who are not actually in schools, are very anxious to huddle safely into the seven or ten per cent or, the ideal haven, the mandatory exceptions. Actually, the more committed a local authority is to promoting interdependence and social justice, the greater the temptation is to have things in there - the mandatory exceptions. But should one school become grant-maintained, it would take a proportion of the mandatory exceptions. It is very important that we look at the expenditure we are putting into the school, not necessarily to diminish it, but to be convinced that it can be allocated to the general schools budget. For example, my belief is that some money for the community should be available; then a contract can be made between community education interests and individual establishments in order to deliver, with mechanisms built in for rewarding 'interdependence activity'. Conversely, there is quite a lot to be said for putting something into a special school budget, provided, again, that the money is geared back into schools with a requirement to support integration of children with special educational needs.

I predict that preschool and community education will be the growth areas in authorities with imagination over the next ten years, because that is where their creativity will still be allowed, according to present legislation; their room for manoeuvre between the ages of five and sixteen to eighteen is heavily circumscribed. So my plea would be for every local education authority to examine existing projects in minute detail, and make sure that those 'retained' areas are as small as they can be. The decisions made about how to describe the general school budget are very important. Moreover, one must remember that within those two areas it is perfectly legitimate to argue that any school thinking of becoming grant-maintained would not take that allocation with it.

INSPECTION

There is obviously going to be a vast increase in the management of small establishments, and we need to think about inspection and how this is to be carried out. A school experiencing multifaceted change and getting it wrong is going to opt out of inspection, particularly if it has ever experienced the kind of inspection that just takes a hard look and produces a report, rather than the kind that tries to look, plan and implement. If schools are able to take their section of the money and buy in, on their terms, the kind of inspection they want there seem to be several hints here for local education authorities. They need to resist the temptation to turn themselves into heavy inspection, quality assurance squads, and perhaps think more carefully about providing a menu from which schools can buy in what they want in terms of inspection - as opposed to what they are required to have. If they do not do that, again more schools may be tempted to become grant-maintained for the wrong reasons.

SPECIAL NEEDS

In Oxfordshire, we decided that we did not believe in statements for children with special educational needs. We felt that the schools could be tempted to use those most vulnerable as a bargaining pawn for resources. So we said, 'The big thing is to make sure that some children get extra resources, not connected with the statement. If they have not got a statement they will get extra resources. Schools will not mistakenly get up into a spiral of having ever more statements in order to obtain more resources.' We knew we still had to give a guarantee to parents, but we did it. We had gone a long way towards integration - then along came the 1987 Act.

People said to us, 'These schools are getting terribly worried about their group sizes going down.' We said, 'No problem. We shall deem the percentage of children, because they are integrated, as *though* they have got statements. Then they will count for more and the group size will go up. Schools will be really pleased about it and, what is more, because they have been rewarded they will not be tempted to be exclusive.'

Then along came 'open enrolment' and people said, 'Now you're for it.' We said:

> 'We'll do exactly the same thing - make sure that there is less opportunity to make competition between the schools by limiting the admission size of schools so that all schools appear to have within their reach the notion of success. We will again deem a percentage of children to be children with special educational needs because they are 'worth' three times as much space. Let us also deem community in - and lo and behold, it diminishes the size of the building stock.'

Then they said, 'You're done for now. Local management of schools. You're really done for ...' Well, they may have been right. You can picture what schools might be like. If the children are each worth a sum of money and, on Thursday afternoon, the school is feeling that it has just had enough of the fifteenth member of the Butcher family (you know how incredibly kind schools are and never prejudge the next member of the family!) they will say, 'We will get rid of the

Butcher's child because the Bowyer's child wants to come into the school. That seems a good trade.'

However, we can solve that one because, within the 75 per cent of the age of pupil formula, we will require every school to have a percentage of children who are worth twice the unit. We will also have a small percentage worth three or four times the unit and we will use the 'seven or ten per cent' to reinforce it. In addition, we will use twenty five per cent that is not age-weighted pupil numbers in order to reinforce notions of special justice and show that everything cannot be reduced to a formula. So, if a school is inclined to exclude the Butcher child, we will say to them, 'That's fine but that child is not worth £1500, but £5500, and you pay for that child's education.'

That is what we attempted in Oxfordshire and we were building in, in the small detail of local management of schools, 'inclusive', as opposed to 'exclusive', mechanisms for schools by which schools could operate.

We need to look forward (beyond the incoherence of a system that disintegrates) to the next Education Act. The demands of social justice will strengthen, then we shall debate, refine and admire the words of Temple and Butler and wonder what madness infected our legislators. We shall look to a new Education Act to produce a set of principles, essay some description of principal partners and their rights and responsibilities. It will contain some mechanisms for management and they will be informed by models of successful schools and successful learning. The legislators will realise their duty to bring within the reach of *all* children, whatever their circumstances, the right to attend successful schools. And the whole Act will be no more than twenty pages - a simple testimony to a nation's resolve to trust each other in the privileged and most important task of educating the next generation of citizens.

References

Butler, R.A. (1971) *The art of the possible*, Hamilton, London

PROCESS AND PEDAGOGY
Effective learning and effective teaching

Introduction

'It is not enough to assume that teachers are in a good position to develop new strategies independently on the basis of common professional skills. Cooperative and well-organised effort is needed.' Stenhouse (1975)

Part II contains four chapters covering a rich kaleidoscope of contexts affected by the current process/pedagogy debate. Part II is essentially written with practising teachers in mind. It raises a number of fundamental questions such as: Why do we teach the way we do? Do we need to rethink and update our pedagogy? Who might help us formulate a view of our daily classroom practice? These chapters are also pertinent to those who manage and advise.

The contributions of Galton, Mayne and Wright are rooted firmly in classroom-based research. Galton considers the contribution of research and researchers to the development of an effective theory of pedagogy. He discusses the notion of the reflective practitioner and asks how realistic it is to expect teachers, working under an ever increasing volume of pressure, to evaluate their own practice and to develop accurate hypotheses based on this.

Galton outlines the merits of teachers working with trained consultants who can contribute directly to discussion on process and pedagogy. He does not denigrate 'action research', as a strategy to increase teacher effectiveness, but cautions overdependence on this approach. Teachers need to find ways of integrating what they learn through their own experience with what is discovered through more formal research methods. Galton illustrates a possible approach by reference to the work of the ORACLE research in primary classrooms. In describing this work he poses fundamental questions relating to the status of the researcher and the appropriateness of the researcher working as a consultant seeking to influence the methodology of teachers in classrooms.

Wright's paper probes a most sensitive area and certainly throws into sharp relief the issue of the researcher working with and reporting on teacher behaviour. Drawing from the findings of classroom observation and interviews with students and teachers Cecile Wright paints a vivid picture of the experiences of black children consequent upon deficiencies in the school system. Racism and the failure on the part of teachers to value black children combine in a powerful causal cocktail which goes a long way to explain the British phenomenon of the underachievement of black children. The chapter also highlights institutional racism which is manifested in the predominance of black students in lower streams, bands and sets. Just how far these discriminatory practices are embedded in our schools is a question as yet unanswered but one which teachers and senior management have to ask of their own school or college situation. This chapter points to a clear need for all those who work in schools to be aware of racist attitudes and actions and to be prepared to develop an individual and institutional code of behaviour to combat such unacceptable conduct.

A-level remains essentially a commodity not a process, and course delivery continues to be dominated by content and providing students with 'a safe set of notes'. HMI paint a depressing picture of a pedagogy characterised by didactic teaching, an absence of variety and passive learning. In less than half of the A-level classrooms observed by HMI was work considered to be 'challenging and scholarly' (HMI, 1988). This is predominantly the result of the failure of teachers to differentiate between examination and teaching syllabuses. Hence teaching tends to be geared exclusively to narrowly conceived examination syllabuses with little reference to the broader aims of post-sixteen education and the needs both of 'young people in transition to adult roles' and of the economy and society.

Mayne's stimulating chapter strikes at the heart of the process/pedagogy debate in a little-studied area of the curriculum. In arguing passionately for A-level teachers to review their classroom process, the writer's concern is to increase the range and quality of learning experiences in A-level classrooms and to maximise opportunities for effective learning. Mayne believes that pedagogy in the A-level classroom is an issue long overdue for professional reflection and development. The chapter is based on the findings of empirical research on the perceptions of teachers and students on the strategies deployed to transact A-level courses. Mayne demonstrates clearly that not only do students and teachers see classroom events differently but so too do members of different subpopulations of students: male, female, ethnic minorities (Asian). The A-level classroom is a far more complex learning environment than commonly recognised by the teachers who work there. In a situation where teachers focus their attention on content and outcomes and employ a pedagogy which is predominantly whole-class in mode, it is barely surprising that they fail to recognise the phenomena of differential perception and experience, and accommodate these in any planned way. If learning in A-level classrooms is to become more effective teachers will need to deconstruct their habitual ways of working, and allow pedagogy to become a legitimate and crucial subject for study and discussion.

The final chapter in Part II differs from the others in not being based directly on specific empirical research. It is nevertheless relevant to the theme of process and pedagogy. Alec Fisher provides a refreshing look at the critical thinking movement which originated in North America, where it has grown rapidly. It is now, of course, also well established in Europe. In fact it is not so much a movement as a number of related experiments which share the objective of improving reasoning and thinking skills in learners by direct method, that is methods designed specifically for that purpose. Reference is made to its historical roots from Socrates through to Dewey. Fisher also highlights the specific contribution of Lipman, whose work is particularly well known in this area, and also that of Paul.

Most would agree that any strategy designed to meet the objective of improving thinking skills must be worthwhile. However, there is debate and disagreement about the transferability of the methodology from one subject to another. Whereas there is clear professional consensus to encourage children to think for themselves, what counts as critical thinking may differ from subject to subject. Fisher concludes by discussing the criticisms of McPeck and his concept of reflective scepticism.

The chapters contained in Part II address issues that are important for all who work in the education system today and provide a stimulus for professional reflection and debate. There is a broad consensus that study and discussion of classroom process is crucial to the effectiveness of learning and to the professional development of teachers. Such study is not an isolated activity in which individual teachers engage but part of a corporate approach to the management of learning within schools and departments. It is not only an issue of honing techniques and strategies to maximise effective learning, but also of arriving at shared values and of translating the aims and aspirations of a school into the daily experience of learners and the practice of teachers.

References

HMI, (1988) *Secondary Schools: An Appraisal by HMI* para. 110, p. 29. HMI, London.

Stenhouse, L. (1975) *An Introduction to Classroom Research and Development*, Heinemann Educational Books, London.

Chapter 5

The implications of recent research on teaching for educational excellence

Maurice Galton

Sylvia teaches nine year old pupils in a primary school in Leicestershire. She is taking part in the STAR project (Science Teacher Action Research), a jointly funded programme of research into science teaching, supported by the Lever-hulme Trust and co-directed by myself and Professor Wynne Harlen, of the School of Education at the University of Liverpool. The STAR project reflects a process approach. The project aims to work collaboratively with teachers allowing them to apply ideas about science teaching in ways that reflect the particular context in which they work. The researchers act as consultants in this process and the teachers are expected to reflect upon their own practice, to suggest hypotheses that might explain the consequences of the lesson and to put forward future schemes of action to see how far these hypotheses could be substantiated and generalised to other classrooms.

THE STAR PROJECT: EXAMPLE

In the particular lesson that I wish to discuss, Sylvia organised the class to work together in groups in order to plan an investigation. The groups had to suggest reasons why a dish of water when placed over a heated surface (a radiator) was gradually reduced in volume (the phenomenon we know as evaporation). The question the children had to address in their group was, 'Where did the water go?' Each suggestion had then to be tested out by planning an appropriate experiment.

Sylvia's account of this lesson was that the children did not cooperate very well. There was too much fooling around. The children quickly wandered away from the point of the discussion, often seemed bored and uninterested in the activity. Neither did they appear to be clear as to what the purpose of the discussion was supposed to be in spite of being told several times.

Sylvia concluded that the task was too difficult for the children and that they needed more guidance from her. Accordingly she set up a repeat of the activity, but this time only one group at a time were involved in science. This enabled her to be present for considerable periods during the initial discussion, directing the group and keeping them to the objectives of the task. Her conclusion, after this second cycle of action research, was that the discussion had been much better, that the students achieved their objectives and that therefore this kind of high-order scientific activity was not one that could be left to children to do on their own. As such, Sylvia seems to have achieved the main objectives of an action research approach. She has developed a hypothesis about her teaching, has tested this hypothesis and found that it was supported by her subsequent observations. Her conclusions were largely unchallenged by her peers who were also participating in the project. There, the matter might have ended but for the consultant who was extremely unhappy with Sylvia's conclusion. The unhappiness arose as a result of several concerns. First, Sylvia's conclusion conflicts with the consultant's own view concerning primary science teaching. The consultant believes that science activities, involving such processes as planning experiments, are ideal when children are working independently of the teacher. Indeed the consultant believes that unless the children regard the ideas that they produce as their own rather than something provided by the teacher they will not be motivated to continue with their experiment should their initial hypothesis prove to be false. The consultant believes that research based upon classroom observation supports his view.

The consultant, as a trained psychologist, is also aware of certain problems that can arise when teachers hypothesise about their own practice. To begin with there is the effect of attribution theory. This states, in its simplest terms, that when we experience failure we often attribute the cause of that failure to circumstances that lie outside our own control. We then have no responsibility for correcting the failure. Thus, faced with the children's inability to engage in a sensible discussion about the planning of their experiment, Sylvia decides that the cause of the problem lies with the children themselves, their inability, at this age, to handle such a complex discussion on their own. This attribution effect can be very powerful. In a study, published in the United States by Beckman (1976) 164 teachers were questioned about the inability of their students to engage in discussions that involved higher cognitive interactions. Not one teacher in the sample explained the failure in terms of *their own teaching*.

The second problem facing Sylvia in her attempt to analyse her practice can also be linked to teachers' attributions about causes of their failure. At Leicester we have called this second effect the 'perception gap in teaching' which stems from the distinction that the famous psychologist, Gordon Allport (1966) noted between *coping* and expressive behaviour. For Allport, *coping* behaviour was a rational response to a particular event in contrast to expressive behaviour that stemmed largely from one's internalised emotional response. Teachers' explanations of classroom behaviour are often likely to be based upon explanations that rationalise events and thereby avoid any consideration of the internal emotional 'turbulence' that the activity in the classroom might have provoked. To take Sylvia as an example, the inability of children to work within a group raises all sorts of emotional concerns for the teacher. Are the children doing work, are they making too much noise, does the teacher in the next room hear this noise and make a judgement about one's competence because it is assumed that such noise indicates a lack of control? Thus, an alternative hypothesis is that Sylvia prefers directing the science activity because it is safer - she feels more in control. Such concerns may have been experienced by Sylvia in the incident discussed earlier, but they would have been unlikely to emerge in any subsequent discussion with the consultant, unless the consultant was prepared to abandon his/her role as facilitator, reflector of ideas, etc. and to take a more directive approach.

Those who argue for the use of the action research approach as the principal method of improving practice would regard the above description as a parody of the activity. Stephen Kemiss asserts that:

> 'The improvement of practice, understanding the situation through action research, requires a spiral of such cycles in order to bring action under control of understanding, in order to develop and inform practical judgement, and in order to develop an effective control of the situation' (Grundy and Kemiss, 1980, p. 85).

In the example cited of Sylvia's classroom, the cycle had only gone through one loop. Kemiss and others would argue that with the support of a skilled consultant and further investigation Sylvia would have come to see that there were other possible solutions to her problem that required her to change both the classroom environment and her own behaviour. There are, however, serious practical limitations with this strategy. First, there is the problem of timescale. In both projects where I have used an 'action research strategy' we have only just got to the stage of completing the first cycle by the end of the three-year funding period. Two recent British publications describing teachers' attempts at engaging in action research - John Nixon's *A Teacher's Guide to Action Research* (1981) and Hustler *et al.*'s, *Action Research in Classrooms and Schools* (1986) - both contain a large number of chapters describing the enthusiastic efforts of teachers to research their own classroom. But one is left, after reading these accounts, with a view of little progress by any of the participants in clarifying theoretical perspectives which, in Grundy and Kemiss' (1981) terms would 'bring action under the control of understanding' and which 'might inform practical judgement of other teachers in similar situations'. Nixon was writing about work carried out in the late 1970s while Hustler describes work undertaken in the mid-1980s. Progress in this area appears, therefore, to be painfully slow.

A second problem, particularly when action research is used to sustain school-based curriculum development, concerns the personalities of those who are likely to engage wholeheartedly in the enterprise. The late Lawrence Stenhouse, in his highly influential book, *An Introduction to Curriculum Research and Development* (1975), described the qualities demanded of the teacher who sought to become his/her own researcher. Such people had to be 'open', 'flexible', amenable to 'criticism' from colleagues and constantly prepared to question their own practice as a way of seeking its improvement. In other words, action research in Stenhouse's terms is not so much an activity but 'a way of life' for the teacher. Almost inevitably, however, teachers who exhibit such characteristics need to reflect similar attitudes in their dealings with their pupils (Stenhouse, 1975, p. 155). They will, in the jargon of American research on teacher effectiveness be committed to 'open learning' environments rather than direct instruction approaches. This particularly applies to primary practice where such views can often be polarised within the school; and indeed, Stephen Rowlands (1982) in his description of one such project readily acknowledges the difficulty of including teachers within the group who do not share the general liberal 'progressive' ideology which underpins the action research approach. There is a danger, therefore, that when a group of teachers work together in this way there may be polarisation of attitudes such that the very act of engaging in open critical discussion by one group of teachers closes them off to the influences of colleagues. As the group becomes more committed and develops a sense of ownership, they then become strongly defensive in the face of criticisms or suggestions from other groups who do not share the prevailing ideology of the action research programme.

It is not my intention to denigrate action research as a vehicle for improving teacher effectiveness. Anyone who has met with teachers who have worked closely with the likes of Stephen Kemiss, John Elliott and the late Lawrence Stenhouse, cannot but be impressed by the sense of commitment and enthusiasm for improving their teaching that these practitioners display. What I am seeking to do here is to identify possible ways of overcoming what I see as two major problems in the approach. The first concerns the timescale that moves from this point of increased commitment to serious reflection leading to the development of more generalised theories about teaching; the second concerns the ways in which this commitment can be extended to colleagues in a school who do not favour these kinds of investigative approaches to classroom practice.

In the United Kingdom those who advocate an action research approach for the improvement of teaching tend to polarise 'reflection in action' as a means of developing theory (Schon, 1983) with models derived from empirical psychological research. For example, in a recent article Kroath (1989) describes an exchange approach whereby researchers attempted to persuade teachers to replace 'the deficient elements in their subjective theory' with formal psychological theory as a basis for changing practice. Kroath reports, however, that the experiment made no impact on the teachers' 'subjective' theory and that teachers reported they did not intend to change any aspect of their theory although they found the exercise a 'stimulating experience' (Kroath, 1989). As described by Kroath, the exercise does not appear to be a very sensitive way of introducing teachers to possible weaknesses in their own thinking which, I have argued earlier, arise out of problems to do with attribution theory. Nevertheless, Elliott

(1989, p.95), in commenting on Kroath's experience, concludes that the approach failed because it encouraged teachers to see teaching as a 'technical rational activity of applying instrumental rules derived from theory rather than as a moral activity of realising values in the activity as a whole'. Elliott's conclusion seems a depressing one for it appears to argue that research on teaching based on empirical studies of classroom process has little to contribute to the development of teachers' thinking about their own practice, unless such teachers have arrived at the point in their own development where they, themselves, see the need for this theoretical input. This is a depressing conclusion because it appears to offer us no solution to the problems discussed earlier concerning the timescale of change and the resolution of views held by different groups of teachers relating to different ideological perspectives.

CONFLICT AND TENSION IN DIFFERENT IDEOLOGICAL THEORIES

In the second half of this chapter, therefore, I want to explore this tension that exists between different kinds of theory. If Kroath is correct and the teacher rejects the psychological theory because it does not accord with their own experience or, as I have suggested, because the very act of being open then leads to one being closed to other influences because of the effects of attribution theory, then how can we integrate what we learn through our own experience with what is discovered through more formal research methods?

I suggest that theories about teacher effectiveness have to be derived by integrating information from three sources. First, there is data which is acquired through reflection in action, the action research approach. Second, there is data which is obtained through empirical studies of classrooms, the process-product approach. The principle behind this method, long ago enumerated by Barr (1935), that we should distinguish between effective and ineffective teachers and then study how they differ in action has a large and very successful history. It has, after all, been used repeatedly in medicine, where although doctors have no idea of the reasons why a treatment works, they accept the legitimacy of the effects of the treatment. On this basis they advise their patients to give up smoking in order to reduce risks of cancer and heart disease. Note that the method does not require us to define effectiveness in terms of standardised testing. We could, for example, wish to distinguish between effective and ineffective questioners or to study classrooms where pupils achieved enhanced self-esteem. Any variable or a set of variables can be used to define effectiveness depending on the value system that one brings to the investigation. What is important is that these positions should be clearly stated.

The third way of extending and building a theory of teaching comes through studies of pupils learning under more controlled conditions. This approach is most apparent in the work of Joyce and Weil (1980) and Joyce and Showers (1983). Joyce examines different models of learning that have been derived through experimentation. He then produces vignettes of lessons that portray how a teacher might implement such a theoretical approach in practice. For example, he makes use of Brunner's ideas of concept attainment to describe a lesson where classification is the main teaching approach. In another section, based upon social learning theory, he offers examples of teachers attempting to raise the level of discussion within group work. Joyce's approach is to present such vignettes to teachers, encourage them to try them out and then to modify them in the light of their own experience. This coaching approach is an incremental one so that teachers are encouraged by success in achieving a set of limited goals. Joyce and Showers (1983) argue that 'to be most effective training should include theory, demonstration and practice, feedback and classroom application'.

The challenge, therefore, is to integrate these different approaches so that we do not get teachers reinventing the wheel. At the same time, we wish to avoid the situation described by Elliott (1989), where teachers having reflected on their actions, reject externalised theory because it operates at the rational rather than the emotional level. I want to illustrate a possible approach by reference to the work of the ORACLE research to primary classrooms.

ORACLE research

The ORACLE research, begun in 1975, investigated a range of questions concerning primary practice. We examined what teachers and pupils did in the classroom using both systematic and participant observation approaches. We made use of both formal and informal methods of assessment and also recorded the attitudes of pupils, their motivation and their anxiety, particularly when the pupils moved from primary to secondary stage of education. Because the study was a longitudinal one, extending over three years, we were able to look at questions of teacher style and the stability of that style with different groups of pupils. Our findings are summarised in a series of volumes of which the most influential two were *Inside the Primary Classroom* (Galton, Simon and Kroll, 1980) and *Moving from the Primary Classroom* (Galton and Willcocks, 1983). The most important results to emerge from the study were those concerned with the description of typical classroom practice as contained in *Inside the Primary Classroom*. The most striking feature of the classroom was the asymmetrical nature of interactions of teachers and pupils. In general teachers were found to be interacting with pupils for 80 per cent of observed time, whereas conversely pupils only interacted with the teacher for 16 per cent of the time. When the 18 per cent of the time during which the pupil talked to other pupils was added to the figure for teacher-pupil interaction then typically pupils were found to work by themselves for over two thirds of the day. This situation arose because of the importance given by the teacher to individualising the instruction. For nearly 60 per cent of the day the teacher was working with one pupil at a time, either moving from table to table or sitting at the desk and dealing with pupils in a queue. Paradoxically, although the teacher addressed the whole class for about fifteen per cent of the day this accounted for three quarters of the contact that the pupil had with the teacher. Despite this relative isolation the typical pupil was engaged on task or routine activities, germane to the task, for nearly three-quarters of the time spent in the classroom.

The interactions between teachers and pupils were also of interest. Contrary to the supposed ideology of primary practice that 'teachers never told children anything' but left pupils 'to find things out for themselves' nearly all the teachers' interactions with individual pupils were managerial or to do with information-giving. Rarely did they concern questioning, particularly questioning involving higher order cognitive thinking. To flesh out these figures, observers wrote anecdotal accounts of the classrooms that they visited. Their descriptions support the view that in attempting to interact with thirty pupils while continuing to direct and control the learning process teachers are under an immense amount of stress. To maintain 'busyness' in the classroom, tasks were therefore organised so that pupils could get on without help from the teacher. These tasks consisted either of worksheets, where pupils filled in missing words from a list provided at the bottom, or of drawing pictures and colouring them in after writing their story or doing additional practice examples in mathematics until the slower pupils on the table caught up. All these were common devices used by teachers to reduce the number of children waiting for attention.

Almost ten years later, the publication by Peter Mortimore, of similar research in London junior primary schools showed very close parallels with the ORACLE study. In the report of the ILEA junior school project published under the title, *School Matters* (Mortimore *et al.*, 1987) there was the same emphasis on managerial interactions and working with individual children rather than with groups or with the whole class. The same degree of asymmetry was, therefore, observed whereby teachers spent around sixty seven per cent of their time working with individual pupils, while pupils spent sixty eight per cent of the time working by themselves without any contact with a teacher or with other pupils. Over two thirds of the teachers were observed to make no use of open-ended questions and there were wide variations in the amount of time that different teachers spent in talking to children about task matters. Positive feedback in the form of praise about work was observed very infrequently. The amount of time teachers spent on class interaction was positively correlated with the amount of time teachers spent talking about work which in turn correlated with pupil progress. As in the ORACLE study, the proportion of time spent on communicating with the whole class was also associated with the use of higher order questions and this factor too was strongly correlated with pupil performance.

One puzzling feature of the ORACLE study was that we did not obtain strong relationships between the time that pupils spent on their task and their progress, as found by Mortimore. In the transfer study where both systematic and participant observation were used a reason for this lack of association between time and progress became apparent. In systematic observation, the observer merely records whether a pupil is engaged on the set task or is distracted in some particular way. What the observer cannot do is to estimate systematically the rate of working of pupils when engaged on their task. Participant observation, however, suggested that there was considerable variation between pupils when working in this way. We identified *easy riders* who did the work but very slowly and prolonged such routine activities as getting their books out of their bag, sharpening their pencil, drawing a margin, etc., while another group, the *hard grinders*, worked more determinedly. In some sessions that we observed, although the class appeared to be working there were very different rates among pupils so that whereas one child might have finished a page and a half of writing another had only produced eight or ten lines.

When this behaviour took place at the beginning of a school year or after transfer to a new school it was, as attribution theory predicts, likely that the teacher would explain the pupil's failure to complete the task by saying that 'he/she lacked concentration'. It appeared to us that the observed need for structure which those supporting direct instruction argued was necessary in order to reduce the anxiety among pupils about what they were expected to do, was capable of a different interpretation. Structure was required by the ORACLE pupils, not so much because it reduced potential anxiety, but because it enabled them to plan ways of avoiding work which they did not wish to do. Children, for example, in mathematics spent much time doing examples from worksheets. Easy riding was a device for planning their work (they planned to make the first worksheet last as long as possible so that they did not have to start a second one).

Pollard, (1985) describes similar phenomena. He identifies different types of pupil and argues that such behaviours are a way of negotiating for a 'working consensus' between the pupils and the teacher which protects each party's 'interests at hand'. Chief among the pupils' interests at hand is their self-image. Difficult work, having to answer difficult questions, puts pupils in a position where they can lose face either with the teacher or with their peers. Consequently, although filling in worksheets, or correcting the grammar of a sentence, is perhaps less interesting than writing a story or solving a mathematical problem it is preferred because it makes less demands on the child and is therefore less threatening.

Such an analysis was confirmed in further studies of pupils during the follow-up ORACLE project, *Effective Group Work in the Primary Classroom* (Galton 1990), which took place from 1980 to 1985 and made use of 'action research' approaches. Here cartoon pictures were used to ask pupils to project their ideas onto imaginary characters who were facing typical situations in the classroom, such as working in a group, listening as part of the class or being helped individually by the teacher. Subject matter could also be changed as could the gender of the pupils involved and of the teacher. Most of the comments showed what John Holt earlier described as 'fear of failure'. Pupils talked about answering teachers' questions as being like 'walking on a tightrope'.

We increasingly focused our attention on the problem of how we could solve the pupils' dilemma which was so perceptively analysed by Walter Doyle in his classification of academic tasks (Doyle, 1986). Doyle's proposition is that the more ambiguous the outcome of a task the more risk it carries for pupils. Hence to accept ownership of a high level task carries with it an increased risk of failure and therefore the possibility of a loss of self-esteem. It was clear that although many teachers emphasised to pupils that 'they should learn by their mistakes' this did not carry over into the everyday behaviour during work in class.

My own experience is that we could not have made progress from this point where we identified problems to do with risk and ownership towards solutions based upon psychological theory while I as the consultant remained outside the action. For me, Elliott's distinction between theories derived from research which he regards as *technocratic* and *rational* as against those which arrive from teacher reflection on practice, which he regards as *moral* since they concern an investigation of one's own values with regard to teaching is unhelpful. This is because it appears to deny teachers the use of a vast research resource concerning pedagogy which has now begun to form a very coherent whole. There remains, however, the problem of how to relate the two sources so that the teacher does not feel that his own ideas are being superseded and undervalued, as in Elliott's example. My conclusion is that this only can happen if the researcher/consultant and the teacher/researcher change roles. In the study on group work, the most significant advances came once I had abandoned my role as consultant/researcher and became instead a teacher in the school. Part of this had to do with a developing relationship because I was a continual physical presence in the school rather than someone who came in in order to observe or to discuss the teachers' reflections. More importantly it was a 'humanising' and 'equalising' experience because the teachers gained an immense degree of confidence from the fact that I was a less skilled practitioner, and that in many instances I failed to achieve as good results in terms of the pupils' behaviour or work as they did. Thus they found that they needed to support me rather than the other way round.

For me the most important aspect of the changed role was that I could study the teachers' and pupils' behaviour on a day-to-day basis as a member of the subculture, as well as analysing my own actions. More importantly, as my own relationship with the children developed, I began to get some insights into the way in which they viewed school and their teachers, insights that I would not have got from questionnaires or interviews. What helped me here, however, was my knowledge of the relevant research so that I knew the likely areas where, for example, fear of failure would be prevalent, such as, reading aloud, discussion in groups. I could therefore target my observations into key areas. More importantly, I now found myself critically questioning some of the practices of the school, particularly as they related to management and behaviour.

As I wrote my diary, having had the benefit of working alongside experienced participant observers in earlier ORACLE studies, I could gradually begin to focus on key questions and formulated the hypothesis that the basic problem in questions of risk lay in the dual messages that teachers were conveying in matters of learning and behaviour. Put simply, teachers were giving pupils the message 'when it's about learning you must do as you think, but when it's about behaviour you must do as I say'. Pupils were, however, unable to make this distinction. To them the teacher was the teacher and when the teacher was talking to them they did not know which role she or he was acting out. Thus pupils did not distinguish between when they were being asked a complex question to which they would be rewarded by praise if they attempted an answer, and on other occasions when an incorrect answer was rejected because 'you were not paying attention'.

In this way the discussions moved towards examining theories of classroom control, to a rejection of soft behaviourism where in Jennifer Nias' example, teachers talk about being the policeman, the boss figure, the teacher, and movement towards what she calls 'an authentic relationship' where both the teacher and the children are relaxed (Nias, 1988). My own attempts to engage in this kind of negotiation were, at first, a singular disaster as recounted in Galton (1989), but they opened the way for much deeper discussions in which colleagues who wanted to try such negotiations were anxious for guidance from the research in order to lessen some of the traumas involved.

I can, however, only hazard a guess that these changes which were just beginning at the end of a five-year project would have continued to take place. However, at the end of that summer, the headteacher departed to take a new post at advisory level. Three of the key teachers left shortly afterwards to take up posts as deputy headteachers in new schools. Within one term, under the direction of a new headteacher, all experiments in negotiation had ceased and, indeed, strong teacher directed control was once again in evidence with frequent examples of teachers shouting at the children. We still do not understand fully the processes of change nor the factors that can assist and inhibit it and that can see an innovative school quickly regress when circumstances change. Of course, it can be said that the teachers who left to take up more senior posts carried their ideas and their practice with them. While, no doubt, the teachers in their new schools were able to take several shortcuts in arriving again at a similar position with new colleagues that it had taken us five years to reach, the lessons I draw from the experience are that changes in teaching style, in particular, are not likely to shift radically outside a five- or six- year timescale. Whether such timescales are acceptable within the context of the demands made by politicians on teachers and schools is another question.

References

Allport, G. W. (1966) Expressive behaviour, in Semeonoff, B. (ed.) *Personality Assessment*, Penguin Books, London.

Barr, A. (1935), 'The validity of certain instruments employed in the measurement of teaching ability', in Walker, H. (ed) *The Measurement of Teaching Efficiency*, Macmillan, New York

Beckman, L. (1976) Causal attributions of teachers and parents regarding children's performance, *Psychology in Schools* (13), pp 212-218.

Doyle, W. (1986) Classroom organisation and management, in Wittrock, M. (ed.) *3rd Handbook of Research on Teaching*, Macmillan, New York, pp 392-431.

Elliott, J. (1989) Educational theory and the professional learning of teachers, *Cambridge Journal of Education* (19), 1, pp 81-101.

Galton, M. (1990) 'Grouping and group work in the primary classroom' in Rogers, C. and Kutnick, P. (eds) *The Social Psychology of the Primary Classroom*, London, Routledge

Galton, M. (1989) *Teaching in the Primary School*, David Fulton, London.

Galton, M., Simon, B. and Croll, P. (1980) *Inside the Primary Classroom*, Routledge and Kegan Paul, London.

Galton, M. and Willcocks, J. (eds) (1983) *Moving from the Primary Classroom*, Routledge and Kegan Paul, London.

Grundy, S. and Kemiss, S. (1981) Educational action research in Australia: the state of the art, in *Proceedings of the Annual Conference of the Australian Association for Research in Education (AARE)*, Adelaide.

Holt, J. (1984) *How Children Fail*, Revised Edition, Penguin, London

Hustler, D., Cassidy, T. and Cuff, T. (eds) (1986) *Action Research in Classrooms and Schools*, Allen and Unwin, London.

Joyce, B. and Weil, M. (1980) *Models of Teaching*, 2nd Edition, Prentice Hall, Englewood Cliffs, New Jersey.

Joyce, B. and Showers, B. (1983) Transfer of training: the contribution of coaching, *Journal of Education* (163), 2, pp 163-172.

Kroath, F. (1989) How do teachers change their practical theories? *Cambridge Journal of Education* (19), 1, pp 59-70.

Mortimore, P. *et al.* (1987) *School Matters*, Open Books, London.

Nias, J. (1988) Informal education in action: teachers' accounts, in Blyth, A. (ed.) *Informal Primary Education Today*, Falmer Press, London.

Nixon, J. (1981) (ed.) *A Teachers' Guide to Action Research*, Grant McIntyre, London.

Pollard, A. (1985) *The Social World of the Primary School*, Holt, Rinehart and Winston, London.

Rowlands, S. (1982) Teachers studying classroom learning, in Galton, M. and Moon, R. (eds) *Changing Schools: Changing Curriculum*, Harper and Row, London.

Schon, D. (1983) *The Reflective Practitioner: How Professionals Think in Action*, Temple Smith, London.

Stenhouse, L. (1975) *An Introduction to Curriculum Research and Development*, Heinemann Educational Books, London.

Chapter 6

A case of ineffective schooling: black children's experience of the education system

Cecile Wright

INTRODUCTION

A readily discernible theme recurring through the increasing literature on black children's experience of schooling relates to their educational attainment. The past couple of decades have witnessed continuing unease at the scholastic performance particularly of Afro-Caribbean children. Numerous studies since the 1960s have suggested that they tend to achieve less well than children from other ethnic groups at both primary and secondary level. Various documented evidence (which includes the Rampton and Swann Reports), and the views of both black parents and their children strongly suggests that effective learning/schooling is not happening for most black children under the current education system. Rather black children's experience of the current education system is one of mis-education or ineffective schooling.

This chapter considers evidence from my recent research study* which highlights how school practices, procedures and organisation can act as restraints upon the attainment of black children, particularly of Afro-Caribbean background. The evidence is taken from an intensive ethnographic and statistical survey of two multiracial comprehensive schools over a two year period. A cohort of Afro-Caribbean girls and boys from both schools were studied in their fourth and fifth years at school. In addition to extensive classroom observations, assessment data accumulated on each pupil were analysed, along with an examination of the schools' allocation procedures. The observed classroom relationships between the white teachers and the Afro-Caribbean pupils are described below. The pupils' views on their schooling is also documented. Finally the pupils' experience of the school's practices and procedures is examined.

---

* This chapter is adapted from a report to the Department of Education and Science on 'The Educational and Vocational Experience of 15-18 Year Old Young People of Ethnic Minority Groups'.

TEACHERS' ATTITUDES, EXPECTATIONS, AND CLASSROOM INTERACTION

The classroom encounters observed for both schools showed the interaction between the teacher and the individual Afro-Caribbean pupils as frequently characterised by confrontation and conflict. Classroom interaction between the teacher and these pupils often takes the form of the teacher enforcing his or her authority and/or expressing criticism. Moreover, those aspects of classroom life which gave rise to conflict between the teacher and the Afro-Caribbean pupil were observed often to be incidental to the real business of teaching. For instance, some teachers were observed frequently to intersperse their lectures with remarks or jokes regarding the Afro-Caribbean student's ethnicity and physical characteristics. Such an act on the part of the teacher was observed to cause considerable distress to these pupils. Observations suggest that behind the quality of interactions that exist between the teachers and their Afro-Caribbean pupils were the generally adverse attitudes and expectations that the teachers held regarding these pupils. Field notes and the dialogue from one of the lessons observed serve to support this claim.

English language CSE (Miss Simms)

This class of middle ability band pupils was taught English language as a form group. The group comprised three Asian girls, six Asian boys, one Afro-Caribbean boy, six Afro-Caribbean girls, one Chinese boy, three white girls, and eight white boys. There was generally a noisy start to most lessons, and it often took the teacher several attempts to secure silence. However, once silence has been established the pupils usually settled down to work and appeared to show a degree of involvement in the task they were given. The teacher's relationship with the class and in particular between her and some of the Afro-Caribbean girls was often a strained one. As the teacher admits:

> 'I really dislike this group, they are the worst group I have in terms of behaviour and motivation. The problem is, a certain group of students, they make things very difficult. I'm referring to the group of four West Indian girls who sit together. I suppose it's something to do with group dynamics. On their own they are reasonable. This group of girls are always in trouble with other teachers and their parents have constantly to be brought in.'

In addition to perceiving the Afro-Caribbean girls as a threat to her classroom management skills, the teacher also held the Afro-Caribbean girls directly responsible for what she considered to be her inability to establish conducive learning conditions. As she states: 'If this group of Afro-Caribbean girls were not in the class, I feel I'd be able to do a much more effective job with the others...'

Such a deduction on the part of the teacher, it may be assumed, cannot be conducive to enhancing a good teacher-pupil relationship. Indeed, observations show the classroom relations between the majority of the Afro-Caribbean girls in this class and the teacher to be based on frequent open confrontations, which generally took the form illustrated in the following classroom incident:

The teacher was already in the classroom when the pupils arrived for the lesson. The pupils arrived five minutes later than normal because they had been to assembly.

Teacher - 'Sit down quietly 4L.' [Stands at desk waiting for the pupils to settle down]

Teacher - 'Will you all settle down quickly. I've waited long enough. On the board is a comprehension question taken from last year's CSE English language paper. I would like you to work through this question, work in your English folder. I will collect your work for marking at the end of the lesson. Now please get on quietly.'

The pupils work in silence. The turning of pages and a student tapping a pen on a desk are the only sounds. The teacher sits at her desk at the front of the room marking a pile of books. The silence continues for ten minutes; then a chair scrapes as an Asian girl leans forward to talk to the white girl sitting in front; four other pupils begin to talk. There is low level noise in the classroom.'

Teacher [looks up from her marking and barks at the whole class] - 'Right, quiet please and get on with your work.'

The silence resumes, and is then broken by an Asian girl talking aloud to an Afro-Caribbean boy.

Kulwinder (Asian girl) - 'Hey Vincent, when will we be having our maths exam?'

Other pupils begin talking amongst themselves. The teacher looks up from her marking as a result of the increasing classroom noise. She looks to the back of the classroom where four Afro-Caribbean girls sit, talking amongst themselves.

Teacher [in a raised voice] - 'Will you four girls stop talking and get on with your work.'

Barbara (Afro-Caribbean) - 'We are working, we're just talking about the question.'

Jean (Afro-Caribbean) - 'It's not only us talking. What about her [pointing to Kulwinder] shouting, why do you always pick on us?'

While the teacher was talking to the Afro-Caribbean girls, three white boys sat playing with a pocket computer game, which the girls had noticed.

Teacher - 'Whenever I look up you're always talking.'

Barbara - 'That's 'cause you only see us, everybody else is talking. Look at them [pointing to the boys playing with the computer game] they're not even working. [Turning to the other Afro-Caribbean girls and talking in a loud whisper] Damn facety.'

The Afro-Caribbeans burst into laughter at Barbara's comment to them.

Teacher [shrilled] - 'Barbara and Jean will you leave the room.'

The girls leave the room, closing the door loudly behind them.'

Teacher [to the class] - 'Will the rest of you settle down now, and get on with your work. I'll be gone for just a few minutes.' [Leavesthe room]

In an interview with the teacher after the lesson, she had this to say about the two Afro-Caribbean girls and the incident which had led her to send them out of the lesson:

'Well I'd say perhaps I have more problems with them than most in the class, perhaps they are the ones whom I'm usually driven to send to Mrs Crane [deputy headteacher] for discipline. I'll put up with so much but they're inclined to become very rude sometimes, which others wouldn't do. They know their limits but those two frequently go over them. It's difficult because I've tried having them sitting separately which doesn't seem to improve things because then they just become very resentful and will try then to kind of communicate across the room, which is almost worse than this business here. As I've said before, they're quite good workers, when they get down to it they enjoy the actual work and they usually get good marks. Their work is generally handed in on time and nicely presented. As I've said, I've sent them out quite frequently and I know lots of other teachers have the same problems. I'm not sure what the solution is. I believe things are being done with them.'

Researcher - 'What happened when you sent Barbara and Jean out of the lesson and you followed them out?'

Teacher - 'I sent them down to Mrs Crane. I told them to take a note and just wait outside her room. They got into so much trouble last term, she [the deputy headteacher] threatened to bring their parents up. I don't know if it actually got to that. I never know quite what to expect, what sort of mood they will be in, they are either in a bad mood or a good mood. Yet I can't tell really, and I find it difficult because I resent having to jolly them along which I do slightly. Because if I just home in on them straight away at the beginning of the lesson and normally they do start their chattering and things right away. Well I try to put up with so much. They react, they just resent it, if I do tell them off. But then I mean they do accept it. In the past when

I've sent them off to Mrs Crane, and after perhaps a blazing row, or having brought her up here [to the classroom], and we have had a big confrontation and I expect them to be quite cool for weeks afterwards, or really rude. And they haven't been at all. Really I have no reason to believe that they would not come in as charming as anything next lesson, or they'll be troublesome, it just depends on them more than me.'

The teacher's conversation, when analysed, provides insight not only into possible factors underlying the incident between her and the Afro-Caribbean girls, but also indicates the criteria used for judging the girls as 'unteachable'.

First, the teacher considers the Afro-Caribbean girls' behaviour in class to be generally unpredictable, as her own comments suggest. She therefore invariably *expected* the girls to be 'troublesome' in class, and as a consequence, also expected to be engaged in frequent confrontation with them. Furthermore, this teacher appeared to use the experiences of other teachers with the girls, both to support and explain her expectations and judgement of them. As a result of her expectations, she was inclined to treat with a degree of suspicion any conciliatory act on the part of the girls towards her following a confrontation as being out of character, and subsequently dismissed.

Second, the teacher considers the girls to be academically able and cooperative in their attitude to work, and this was borne out by observations. Yet from her behaviour towards the pupils it appeared that these features received only secondary consideration from the teacher, compared to the pupils' alleged 'troublesome' classroom behaviour.

AFRO-CARIBBEAN PUPILS' VIEWS ON SCHOOL AND CLASSROOM LIFE

Conversations with the Afro-Caribbean girls and boys in both schools, in an attempt to ascertain their perspectives on school and classroom life and their adaptation to their perceived experiences, suggest that these pupils often wonder whether there is anything more to classroom activity for them than insults, criticisms, and directives.

A discussion with a group of Afro-Caribbean girls in which they talked vividly of their experience of some teachers supports this claim:

Barbara - 'The teachers here, them annoy you, too much.'

Researcher - 'In what ways do they annoy you?'

Barbara - 'They irate you in the lesson, so you can't get to work.'

Group - 'Yeah.'

Barbara - 'One day Mr Beresford gave the class a piece of work to do, I type fairly fast and so I finished first. I took the piece of work to Mr Beresford and told him I'd finished the work, he said that I wasn't the only person in the class and he had to see other children before me. I asked a question on the work and he gave me a funny answer saying 'I should know by using a typist's intuition'. I told him I wouldn't be able to know, if we were told to do straightforward copying, with that he threw the piece of paper at me. I was angry, so I threw it back at him ... In the third year, I did sewing with Mrs Lewis, we got on well until one day, she kept telling me off for talking loud, then she accused me of saying 'How now brown cow' and sent me down to Mrs Crane [deputy headteacher] for discipline. She insisted that I did call it Mrs Lewis, even though I kept telling her I didn't know what it meant and that I didn't even know a verse like that existed. I got sent out of the lesson for the rest of that year, which was about four or five months ... I was thrown out of sewing by Mrs Lewis, out of French for some reason I can't remember why, out of art, for a misunderstanding with the teacher about wiping glue off some scissors, out of office practice about three times for about a period of two to three weeks each time ... I've been in trouble all my school life, I think the girl who I used to hang around with gave the teachers the impression I wasn't worth the bother. I feel some teachers are prejudiced.'

Vera - 'Yeah, I agree with her, take the cookery teacher.'

Susan - 'For example in cookery, there were some knives and forks gone missing, right, and Mrs Bryan goes "Where's the knives and forks?" looking at us lot [the Afro-Caribbean pupils in the class].'

Vera - 'Yeah, all the blacks.

Sonia - 'Seriously right, in the past most coloured children that had left school they've all said she's prejudiced.'

Jean - 'She's told some kids to go back to their own country.'

Sonia - 'Seriously right, if you go to another white teacher or somebody, an' tell them that they're being prejudiced against you, they make out it's not, that it's another reason.'

Jean - 'When Mrs Bryan told Julie to go back to her own country, she went and told Mrs Crane. Mrs Crane said that Mrs Bryan was depressed because her husband was dying.'

Sonia - 'So why take it out on the black people. Then she's told black people to do many things, she even called them monkey.'

Researcher - 'Would you say that the Afro-Caribbean boys have the same experience with the teachers as yourselves?'

Vera - 'The boys I know don't get the same treatment because most of the lads are quicker to box the teachers - than the girls, you see.'

Group - 'Yeah.'

Similarly a group of eight Afro-Caribbean boys were asked about their school and classroom experience. They responded as follows:

Mullings - 'The teachers here are too facety, they don't give you a chance.'

Michael - 'For example Hill [Afro-Caribbean boy] who was expelled.'

Paul - 'That just prejudice, he never did nothing wrong.'

Michael - 'He never done nothin' much you know. He's half-caste, but he was more to the coloured people dem.'

Researcher - 'Why was he expelled?'

Michael - 'What it is I think he got suspended three times and he was on report, kept getting bad grades, they just out him in front of the governors. Yet a big skinhead [white boy] right, he go in front of the governors three times already, right, they expelled him. He came back, and dem let him back in a de school yesterday.'

Paul - 'Teachers look down on you, Mr Parks, Mr Gordon, Mr Henry, Mr Gray, and some others. I can remember the time I was in metalwork, Mr Gray keep saying to me why you've a tan? Why have you got a tan? I say well I've been like this all me life. He say, well you should go back to the chocolate factory, and be remade or something like that [with anger] that's not nice at all.'

Michael - 'One day I was in there [in the classroom] so I don't know what happened between him and Errol, he came up to me and say, "Why Paul, Errol, and Delroy is always giving us hassle" and all that. So I said, "Oh well, you know how Paul and Delroy are, they won't take anything off you lot in'it. If anything, them like to stick up for them rights." So he said to me, "You know I like running a joke, Michael."'

Keith - 'Mr Gray, right, he says it's a complete joke what he says to black kids, he said one day he was at lower school and he came in [the classroom] and said to this girl, this coloured girl was a bit upset, so he said to her "What's wrong with you?" and he said, "I'll have to send you back to Cadbury's to let them wipe the smile off your face" and the girl went home and told her father. And her father took her to the Race Relations Board, and he [Mr Gray] says he's to go to court.'

Keith - 'They don't give the half-caste kids no hassle, no hassle whatsoever. However, if the half-caste kids act black, they pick on them, hassle man.'

Errol - 'And the Asians.'

Group - 'Yeah.'

Researcher - 'Are you all also saying that the Asian students are not treated in the same way by some teachers, as you suggest, the Afro-Caribbean pupils are treated?'

Keith - 'Because with the Asians, right, Asians just keep themselves to themselves like we now, we just want equality with the white people. Asians don't speak their minds, they keep it all in because they are afraid.'

Michael - 'They get fling around, they won't say nothing about it.'

Keith - 'Because of that Asians are better off than black pupils that's all I can say.'

Paul - 'Yeah, Asians aren't the ones what go around causing trouble with the teachers.'

Researcher - 'Are you all saying then, that the Afro-Caribbean or black children, as you put it, go around causing trouble?'

Group [defensively] - 'No, No.'

Keith - 'No, the thing that we want right, we want equality just like the white people, we want equal rights.'

Paul - 'I'm not saying that we cause trouble, but I'm just saying the teachers think black boys are always going around causing trouble. That's what they think.'

Keith - 'Teachers look down on you.'

The Afro-Caribbean boys were asked to explain further how the nature of the relationship which they considered existed between some teachers and themselves affected their behaviour towards these teachers. Using their analysis the pupils felt that they were forced into a stimulus-response situation; as the dialogues that follow demonstrate:

Paul - 'The school don't respect black students. We are treated badly, we are forever hassled. I can remember the time I was in (subject), Mr X keep saying to me "Why you've got a tan?" I say, "Well I was born like this." He say, "Well you should go back to the chocolate factory and be remade," or something like that. To me that wasn't a nice thing to say.'

Kevin - 'We are treated unfairly, because we are black. They look after their flesh not ours.'

Michael - 'They look after them white people-dem, you know what I mean, but we get dash at the back all the time.'

Researcher - 'You have all said that you feel that you are treated unfairly in the school. How do you feel this makes you behave?'

Delroy - 'Bad.'

Researcher - 'When you say 'bad' what exactly do you mean by this?'

Paul - 'It means that we turn around and make trouble for them.'

Delroy - 'Yeah, we try to get our own back on them. We behave ignorantly towards them, and when the teachers talk to us and tell us to do something we don't do it, because we just think about how they treated us.'

Paul - 'Like when you walk down the corridor, and a teacher stops you, you just ignore him. When they stop you for no reason you just irate.'

Researcher - 'How about you, Errol?'

Errol - 'I try to keep out of trouble the best I can. If they cause trouble with me I cause trouble with them it's as simple as that. If you are a troublemaker, right, and you're pretty intelligent, they still keep you down. Look what they've done to Delroy, he's pretty intelligent, yet they keep him down, no wonder he causes trouble. I want to get on so I try to keep out of trouble.'

The Afro-Caribbean girls and boys in their conversations seem to be expressing similar complaints and dissatisfaction regarding their teachers' attitudes and behaviour towards them. Certainly similarities were observed in the way in which they responded to their teachers' treatment of them. For instance, in the classroom they were both prepared to openly confront and challenge the teacher, using Jamaican patois in their exchanges with the teacher. In this situation some teachers felt quite threatened by the pupils' use of a dialect they could not understand. The teachers' anxiety served only to accentuate their negative attitudes and behaviour towards those pupils who used patois. For the Afro-Caribbean pupils the use of a mode of communication outside the cultural repertoire of the teacher is intended to undermine the teacher's authority. In many instances this strategy was observed to be quite effective.

Another way in which the Afro-Caribbean pupils, particularly the boys, responded to the poor relationship which existed between them and their teachers was to organise into a large all Afro-Caribbean group which moved around the school at break time baiting the teachers and subjecting them to a barrage of patois. In the words of one pupil the purpose of their behaviour was to 'get our own back for what they [teachers] do to us'. Moreover, in behaving in this way, these pupils also entered into a self-fulfilling prophesy, which further appeared to justify the teachers' expectations of them.

THE OUTCOME OF THE AFRO-CARIBBEAN STUDENT-TEACHER RELATIONS

As argued so far the relationship between teachers and Afro-Caribbean pupils within both schools was often antagonistic. There is evidence to suggest that the quality of this pupil-teacher relationship may precipitate certain sanctions taken by the school against these pupils, the ultimate sanction being the removal of students from the school. Data examined on the suspension and expulsion for the year group studied for both schools reveal a higher proportion of suspension and expulsion amongst Afro-Caribbean pupils, even though they constituted the smallest ethnic group. In one school, for instance, over half the students from this year group suspended or expelled were Afro-Caribbean. In addition to this it was found that none of these pupils expelled from the school in the fourth year were offered alternative education provision, signifying that these pupils were thus entirely without formal education. Indeed, in the Afro-Caribbean students' conversations above, the issue of suspension and expulsion is emphatically discussed indicating how very real this issue is to their experience of schooling.

Another way in which the Afro-Caribbean students were also found to be denied educational opportunities as a consequence of the adverse relationship between them and their teachers, stemmed from what was found to be their teachers' faulty assessment of their abilities and achievements. Evidence suggests that in their assessment of the Afro-Caribbean pupils the teachers allowed themselves to be influenced more by behaviour criteria than cognitive ones. That is, the assessment given would be most likely to reflect the teachers' subjective involvement with the complex behavioural aspects of classroom relations. This in turn led to a situation where Afro-Caribbean students, more so than any other pupil groups, were likely to be placed in ability bands and examination sets well below their actual academic ability. This indicates that in their assessment of the Afro-Caribbean pupils' ability the teachers were less able to exercise professional judgement.

The apparent misplacement of the Afro-Caribbean pupils on the basis of their ability, would strongly suggest that within this school overt discriminatory practices were operating against the Afro-Caribbean students. This suggestion is supported by the view of one of the teachers, when attention was drawn to the placement of an Afro-Caribbean pupil in a CSE French examination set who otherwise, on the basis of her ability, should have been placed in an O-level set. 'This pupil has been on the fringe of trouble all year, her attitude to the teachers is not at all good, she can be a nuisance in class.'

It seems obvious from this teacher's statement that ability is a positive quality in some teacher's eyes, only if it is shown by a white, and possibly an Asian pupil.

Certainly, the Afro-Caribbean pupils in their conversations expressed anger that the teachers had low expectations of their abilities and in some cases prevented them entering for certain public examinations. However, they were optimistic that they would be able to undertake the courses at the college of further education, denied them by the school, as the following student's comment would appear to suggest:

'I've been entered for all CSEs: typing, maths, English, social studies, and art. I haven't been entered for office practice and French. For office practice it was my teacher's decision. She said that I didn't have enough pieces of course work [project] to be recommended, even though a friend [white girl] of mine has less pieces of work and has been entered. I do feel a bit bitter about it but I've decided I will retake it when I go to college.'

An analysis of the overall attainment in the public examinations (that is CSEs and O-levels) for all the pupils in the year group studied for both schools was undertaken. Figures show that the proportion of Afro-Caribbean pupils entered for, and thus gaining O-levels, was dramatically lower than for the Asian and white pupils. The educational attainment for the Afro-Caribbean pupils is particularly alarming when it is realised that in one of the schools the Afro-Caribbean pupils (for the year group studied) entered the school at eleven plus with an average reading age slightly above the whole intake for the year.

It is evident from the findings in this chapter that within the classroom, in allocation to sets, streams, or bands, and in examination entries, complex processes may be involved which serve to disadvantage black pupils, particularly those of Afro-Caribbean origins. Moreover, it is clear that assignment of pupils to groups undertaking a lower standard of work than they are capable of, and in turn entering them for lower level examinations or no examinations at all can affect the type of school-leaving qualifications attained.

The weight of evidence in this chapter highlights an experience of schooling which clearly places black children at a disadvantage in the education system. This situation is reflected in the minutiae of classroom interactions (particularly teacher-pupil interaction), the structures, policies and practices of the school. If black children are to benefit fully from the education system, therefore, it needs to be acknowledged that a reform of education, or alternatively a transformation of education is necessary. A transformation at the personnel and structural end is particularly desirable. This begs the question, whether the provision of the 1988 Education Act is the answer for the desired changes required to improve the educational opportunity of not only black children, but all children.

References

Eggleston *et al.* (1985) *The Educational and Vocational Experience of 15-18 Year Old Young People of Ethnic Minority Groups'*, DES, London.

Wright, C.Y. (1985a) 'Learning environment or battleground?', in *Multicultural Teaching*, Trentham Books Ltd, Stoke on Trent

Wright, C.Y. (1985b) 'Who succeeds at school - and who decides?', in *Multicultural Teaching*, Trentham Books Ltd, Stoke on Trent

Wright, C.Y. (1987) 'Black students - white teacher', in *Racial Inequality in Education*, B. Troyna (ed.), Routledge and Kegan Paul, London.

Chapter 7

Effective learning: pedagogy in the 'A' level classroom

Peter Mayne

In a fascinating paper published at the beginning of the 1980s Brian Simon, a fellow contributor to this volume, explored the question 'Why no pedagogy in England ?' In contradistinction to other European states no clear science of teaching has developed in this country. As a result historically 'our approach to educational theory and practice has tended to be amateurish and pragmatic' (Simon, 1981). In the absence of professional consensus on how students learn and the ways in which effective student learning can be facilitated, teaching has developed as an individualist and isolated classroom activity where practice has been conditioned by mores - sometimes reflecting the teachers' own experience as a child - mediated by the realities of everyday curriculum transaction. Until quite recently in many schools learning and teaching styles have thus been low on the agenda for professional discussion between colleagues.

As we enter the 1990s, however, there are signs that a sea change is in process - at least in the five to sixteen phases of education. This is in part the result of specific initiatives such as national curriculum key stages, GCSE, TVEI, and records of achievement, as also of environmental changes consequent upon the 1986 and 1988 Education Acts. 'The increasing involvement of governors, parents and members of communities in discussion about the curriculum ... emphasises the importance of clarifying the teachers' responsibility for the curriculum.' This lies first and foremost in the domain of pedagogy (The Leicestershire LEA Curriculum Statement, 1988). Furthermore, the sheer pace of change in the second half of the 1980s has created a situation in which teachers - *in extremis* - have been forced to work together in devising new teaching and learning styles. Perhaps the days of the amateur, pragmatist and isolationist are waning at last as lay opinion acknowledges the complexity of curriculum and pedagogy and teachers themselves acknowledge that they 'develop professionally when they refine their knowledge about pedagogy by observing and reflecting upon their experience in organizing students' learning in classrooms' (The Leicestershire LEA Curriculum Statement, 1988).

While the curriculum experience of pre-sixteen students has changed quite radically, traditional sixteen to nineteen work has remained in something of a time warp. At its best, thinking about the eleven to sixteen curriculum is holistic.

Experiences are viewed within a coherent framework of entitlement. Principles - such as breadth, coherence, balance, relevance and differentiation - overarch the whole curriculum and infuse its components. This necessitates planning and management at both the whole school and department level. By contrast, evidence of such coherent management of A-level programmes and experiences is rare, even at the course or department level. While syllabus content and resources are a common feature of departmental discussion teaching and learning styles are not, even in colleges specializing in sixteen to nineteen work. My own research failed to locate any whole establishment discussion whatsoever on this topic (Mayne, 1988). It is as if the profile of pedagogy as an issue of professional concern declines in a negative correlation to the increase in the age of students encountered.

Advanced level work is prized by teachers, schools and government alike as a flagship provision, a marker of quality in the system. However, the status of A-level lies in its outcome, its value as a negotiable commodity rather than in the inherent quality of student experience on A-level courses. This is demonstrated starkly in a recent statement by university history departments. While 'they were not discontented with A-level as an entrance exam ... their confidence did not extend to history as currently taught' (*Times Educational Supplement*, 1989). This absurd disconnection between process and product helps to explain why A-level pedagogy remains both low on the agenda and at the margins of legitimacy for discussion between departmental colleagues. Typically even where teachers share a group, it is deemed unnecessary for them to discuss the methods each employs to transact the course (Mayne, 1988). HMI (1984) reporting on the work of one sixth-form college noted:

> 'Teaching styles for A-level are highly individual and widely contrasting ...
> They range from a rather narrow coaching method to the open-ended
> scholarly approach ... There is evidence that students find this dichotomy
> confusing and there is urgent need for some coordination of approaches ...
> Much more needs to be done both in the College as a whole and in individual
> departments to diagnose student needs, to develop teaching strategies to
> meet them and to use teaching time more flexibly.'

The professional autonomy of individual A-level teachers to determine the way in which they work with their groups is prized as an important feature of sixth form work (Mayne, 1988). The guarded language of HMI (1988a) in stating what in other contexts might be seen as the obvious may result from their acknowledgement of this prevailing view. 'Departmental and other discussions of teaching method and assessment,' they comment 'could help to improve the planning and conduct of the work ... A common departmental policy on teaching objectives, methods and appropriate means of review and assessment is desirable' (HMI). This chapter takes a more forthright stance. Nowhere is the need for change post-sixteen more apparent than in the pedagogy used in A-level course delivery. A-level students experience a curriculum diet all too often characterised by passive, whole-class and undifferentiated learning styles with limited variety of pedagogic fare. This is supported by the findings of HMI in their surveys of A-level work in the mid 1980s:

> '... in more than half the lessons seen in sixth forms students spent a considerable proportion of their time as passive recipients of information.' (HMI, 1988b)

> 'the principal objective of many staff and students alike, was the provision of what they regarded as a 'safe' set of notes for revision purposes, and there were examples of teachers engaging in monotonous and extensive exposition, dictating notes or requiring notes to be copied from the blackboard, and of students taking a wholly passive role.' (HMI, 1988a)

> 'Some of the teaching took place in the constant shadow of the examination with a narrow concentration on essay and context questions to the exclusion of other activities, which had the effect of shrouding the vitality of literature in an air of gloomy retribution.' (HMI, 1986)

Individual subjects do not exist in isolation and schools and colleges articulate broader aims for their sixteen to nineteen programmes than academic success and progression to higher education. They acknowledge their students as 'young people in transition to adult roles' and aim to provide a range of experiences to assist this transition. A-level process must reflect these broader aims if they are to be translated into reality. It makes no curriculum sense whatsoever to do otherwise. The history of attempts to deliver breadth and relevance post-sixteen as 'additionality' is strewn with a litany of failed good intentions. 'Consequently where teaching styles concentrate on the transmission of information but neglect these other objectives, they do not serve the students well' (HMI, 1988a)

It is not whole class, directive teaching strategies *per se* but the dominance of these approaches that is criticised here. They do indeed have a proper place within a varied and rich A-level pedagogy which must also include opportunities for students to engage actively in their own learning. Where didactic approaches dominate a classroom ethos develops which 'encourages passive attitudes in students who often appear to lack involvement in or enthusiasm for the subjects being studied' (HMI, 1984). 'A-level,' says Higginson (1988) 'should ... aim to whet the appetite for active learning. Project and practical work, simulation, working with others, discussion and oral presentation can all offer opportunities for students to practise relevant skills and can jolt them out of a passive attitude to learning.'

The lessons of good practice elsewhere in schools demonstrate emphatically that 'good teaching and effective learning necessarily employs a variety of approaches in which students are actively involved, and in which they become progressively more responsible for their own learning' (Warwickshire Education Department, 1989). This should be a significant consideration for A-level teachers planning learning experiences for students who have graduated from

GCSE. As Mitchell (1987) points out 'even where students have chosen a course they can find the course demotivating' if, for example, there is 'an over-emphasis on factual content and insufficient opportunity to make choices about what to study and how to study.'

It is insufficient to allow pedagogy to reside where it does at present, as a non-issue, something which individual teachers determine in isolation. If we are truly concerned about effective learning and a broad and relevant education post-sixteen its profile has to be raised significantly both for teachers and curriculum managers.

THE PROJECT AND ITS FINDINGS

This chapter discusses some of the findings of a study of A-level classroom process undertaken in 1986 (Mayne, 1986). The project sought to describe process within the black box of the A-level classroom: to describe the pedagogic repertoire of the teachers and the incidence of particular teaching strategies and, more importantly, to pose questions about the degree to which A-level teachers actually think pedagogically. Could they describe their pedagogy accurately in terms of the twenty teaching strategies and eleven teacher characteristic variables of the instrument? (see boxes 1, 2). How aware were they, for example, of the degree to which boys and girls viewed their teachers and a supposedly common classroom experience differently? Were the patterns of differential interaction with these groups consciously planned? The results of this enquiry make a tentative contribution to consideration of pedagogy and effective learning in the A-level classroom.

The study used nine establishments with sixth form provision in two areas of the Midlands - schools, and sixth form, tertiary and further education colleges. The sample comprised 452 A-level history and physics students and their 52 teachers. The instrument was administered in the classroom by the researchers. Students and teachers were asked to complete the questionnaire by indicating the frequency that they perceived the variables to occur in their experience of the nominated class over time. Respondents were briefed to confine themselves exclusively to activity in the classroom and physicists were instructed to ignore practical work sessions, which in all but one class visited were organised as discrete timetabled events.

The instrument was designed to permit an analysis of the differential perceptions of A-level classroom process expressed by respondents grouped into populations within the sample. The responses of five paired populations were correlated and a statistical analysis made. The five were: all teachers versus all students, history versus physics students, sixth versus seventh year students, female versus male students, and students classifying their ethnic origin as UK/Irish versus Asian (Indian subcontinent).

Before describing the results of the population analyses it is important to refer briefly to a major finding of the preliminary data analysis which has significant

---

Box 1 - Instrument Section I variables: teaching strategies

1. Teacher dictates notes
2. Students work in pairs or small groups
3. Students use worksheets
4. Teacher gives tests
5. Students ask questions
6. Teacher goes over set work with the whole class
7. Students present prepared work to the whole class as individuals or members of small groups
8. Teacher talks/lectures to the whole class
9. Class discussion takes place
10. Students take notes from books
11. Teacher asks questions
12. Students cover work at their own pace
13. Students actively involved in the lesson
14. Teacher talks with individuals or small groups
15. Individuals or small groups undertake small project/investigation
16. Teacher explains how to approach tasks - for example, topic, homework.
17. Students collaborate in small groups/pairs
18. Teacher moves around the class
19. Students encouraged to show initiative in undertaking tasks
20. Teacher goes over work with individuals or small groups

---

bearing on the substance of the chapter. The discriminant analysis, which was run primarily to test the validity of the instrument, also showed that students in the same group possessed a shared view of the pedagogy employed in their classroom to the extent that students could be allocated to their actual groups on the basis of their responses. This shared view was often at variance with the way in which the teacher sought to describe her pedagogy. In instances where a group was taught by two teachers, students proved competent to describe the experiences of the two classrooms distinctly. Interestingly, where a teacher taught more than one group in the sample she failed to identify the differences in pedagogy that were evident to her students. This would seem to support our contention that consideration of pedagogy at A-level is afforded little time by practitioners and also attests to the rudimentary state of the art of evaluating styles of teaching and learning in the A-level classroom.

Box 2 - Instrument Section II variables: teacher characteristics

a.   Someone who organizes your work for you

b.   Someone who ensures that you do your work

c.   Someone who provides factual information

d.   Someone who assesses your progress

e.   Someone who encourages you to think for yourself

f.   Someone who is a source of guidance

g.   Someone who helps you organize your work

h.   Someone who encourages you to assess your own progress

j.   Someone from whom you expect answers

k.   Someone who encourages you to express your own ideas

l.   Someone who talks to you at your own level.

POPULATION ANALYSES

Teachers and students

It is noted that significant differences in perception existed in respect of ten strategic and ten teacher characteristic items of the instrument. Broadly teachers claimed significantly higher frequencies for non directive, proactive student and group strategies than were perceived by their students. They dictated notes, lectured and presented themselves as providers of factual information to a far greater extent in the eyes of their students than they themselves would admit and they were at variance with their students on the frequency with which they involved students in lessons - even at the level of asking questions and promoting class discussion. Students perceived lower levels of group work, collaboration and student presentations. They saw their teachers interacting with individual students and small groups much less than their teachers indicated. This perceptual difference in the degree to which A-level teaching has a whole class orientation is particularly sharp in answer to the question relating to going over set work. Students clearly perceive this as being done with the whole class; teachers, however, indicate higher frequencies of individual and group strategies.

The bias towards teacher driven rather than student centred approaches is reinforced by subsequent more detailed analysis of the data. Emphatically, it was the experience of students that A-level teachers employ a pedagogy which is didactic, directive and whole class in orientation - the traditional safe route to achieving examination success (HMI, 1988a). This picture of classroom life - albeit demanding major change - is unremarkable in itself given, *inter alia*, recent HMI survey work. What is more interesting, however, is the degree to which teachers and students perceive A-level classroom experience and A-level teachers differently.

In seeking to account for this difference it is possible to argue that the difference is more apparent than real when described in terms of responses to the instrument. In short, that in reality A-level teachers share the student view but they were not prepared to admit to this in their responses. They were in the horns of a professional dilemma. At a time when teachers are encouraged to pose questions about the quality of student learning experience, course aims beyond teaching to the syllabus and the transferability of learning, skills and attitudes which transcend the understandable but nonetheless narrowly mechanistic goal of achieving examination success, the sample teachers claimed higher levels of professionally acceptable strategies than were actually experienced by their students.

In a limited follow up study in which the instrument was discussed with teachers who were not part of the main study, it was clear that market forces and accountability to students, parents and management are keenly felt and impact on A-level practice. Ironically this is a fundamentally different environment from that which spawned the strategies still commonly deployed to transact A-level. In a scenario in which teachers lacked resources, taught many students who were struggling to meet the demands of A-level, and were under pressure from management to raise or maintain examination pass rates it was perfectly understandable that emphasis was placed on giving the students 'a good set of notes'. If teachers are genuinely constrained from reflecting upon their pedagogy and working towards their professional development because of these tensions and inconsistencies in the system we would argue the case again for a whole institution review of teaching and learning styles and a more honest attempt to fuse the broad aims of sixteen to nineteen education with the actuality of curriculum practice in the classroom.

However, the premise underpinning this paper is that the perceptual mismatch described above cannot satisfactorily be explained in terms of the cynically contrived responses of A-level teachers under pressure. In a situation in which the teachers themselves asked for feedback on our findings and where they were conscious that their students were completing the same instrument in an adjacent room there is a limit to the extent to which teachers simply provided professionally conditioned responses. As the researchers had had contact with almost all teacher respondents and their classrooms, the degree to which reality could have been bent was unlikely to reach the point of absurdity. In some departments there was a prevailing ethos of safe didacticism; the extent to which teachers here, having outlined their approach in discussion, would then refract reality in their questionnaire responses is surely limited. Therefore while acknowledging that these pressures were undoubtedly operating, the effect of their mediation was insufficient in itself to produce a rogue result. A significant gap does exist between what teachers intend and indeed perceive to occur in their classrooms and what students experience there. When traditional yardsticks for evaluating A-level practice remain the essentially product-orientated ones of pass rates and completion, *per se*, of a content-laden syllabus it is barely surprising that the process considerations of pedagogy and learning styles remain largely unconsidered.

The analyses which follow concern the perception of student subpopulations and demonstrate clearly that they perceive their classroom experience differently. This raises pertinent questions about evaluation of pedagogy and intention in the classroom and the degree to which teachers are conscious of the pattern of differentiation described below. Teachers might like to ask themselves whether their approaches to, for example sixth and seventh year, or male and female students, are different, and if they are intentionally so, whether the differences perceived by students are the ones they are meant to experience. There is a strong case, it would appear, on these points alone for teaching and learning styles to figure more prominently in the shared concerns of A-level teachers and curriculum managers at the department and institution level.

History and physics students

Writing about history teaching in the sixth form Stephen Pam commented:

> 'In the past ... teaching at A-level has been notoriously poor. Sixth formers have unquestioningly accepted and noted down a mass of facts and opinions from their teachers, to reproduce them in answer to examination questions ... This method certainly works in so far as it leads to examination success, but it is ... educationally indefensible' (Pam, 1984).

In conducting the research we sought to test on the one hand the degree to which the A-level subjects chosen had characteristic pedagogies and on the other the degree to which teachers used a traditional pedagogy to deliver A-level courses which was fundamentally similar irrespective of subject for most of the time. To test this we excluded the subject-specific practical component of physics by restricting physics students and teachers to describing 'non practical' or 'theory' lessons. While students said that they felt perfectly able to make this distinction when they were given the questionnaire we have no way of knowing how successful they were in so doing.

It would appear from our results that the student experience of A-level teaching strategies in the two subjects studied was distinct, although given the nature of these differences it would be interesting to ascertain the degree to which these were intentionally so and to canvass subject teachers' views on whether the resulting pictures are ones by which they would wish to be characterised.

While only four significant differences, existed when seventh year student responses were analysed, this increased greatly to twenty one for the sample as a whole. It would appear that the imminence of the A-level examination tends to produce a common pedagogy and to pale differences in subject delivery.

Seventh year historians saw their teachers more as a source of guidance than their physics peers, more likely to advise how to approach tasks and to organise work. Such guidance was offered to the whole class.

Taking the sample as a whole history teachers were described as whole class operators: lecturing, questioning and directing discussion. Even when history teachers went over set work this was done for the whole class, whereas the physics teacher would work with groups or individuals. Physics teachers were more mobile in the classroom and worked with individuals and small groups more frequently. Although historians recorded a higher incidence of group and individual presentations to the class, preparatory work had been done outside the classroom.

When described in terms of student responses to section II variables history and physics teachers appear differently. Broadly speaking the former were seen as helpful sources of guidance and encouragement and more was expected of them than of physics teachers by their students. History teachers were clearly felt by their students to be significantly more a source of information and guidance than were physics teachers. Historians helped students organise their work and played a disciplining role in ensuring that work was completed on time. They also spoke to their students significantly more frequently at what their students considered was an appropriate level.

Sixth and seventh year students

Sixth and seventh year students were questioned in their third and fifth term of A-level study respectively. The two year groups saw significant differences in the way their teachers worked with them. Teachers might like to reflect therefore on the congruence of planned differences in approach with consumer perception.

In all, fourteen strategy items were found to differ significantly. The pattern for year six was more directive and whole class, with on the one hand a higher incidence of dictated notes and use of worksheets and on the other less testing, discussion and group work. Teachers of year six classes were seen as less mobile, interacting less frequently with individuals or groups of students and characterised as providers of information. They were also seen communicating at an appropriate level with their students. Given that year six students were given questionnaires after almost a year's experience of A-level work these differences are intriguing. The low incidence of testing and the high value allotted to information transmission in year six pose interesting questions about planning of a two-year course, as does the powerful skewing towards testing in year seven.

Female and male students

The student sample comprised forty one per cent female students distributed between history and physics in a ratio of approximately 3:1. Significant differences in male-female perception existed in several strategy and characteristic items. When compared to their male peers, the girls perceived a significantly lower incidence of teacher interaction with individuals and of individual and small group work and a higher incidence of whole-class strategies. As the majority of teachers in the sample were male (sixty two per cent) this raises issues about the way in which male teachers support the learning of their female students in class. This is particularly important in a situation in which teachers operated predominantly in a whole class mode and were unconscious of any differentiation in their behaviours towards male and female students in their classes. Given the predominance of a whole-class, directive pedagogy it is curious that girls considered that there were significantly fewer opportunities provided for them to work at their own pace than perceived by the boys.

Section II responses indicate that female students viewed their teachers as more central to their learning than did their male peers. Hence the girls saw their teachers more as a source of guidance, information and help in organizing their work than did the boys.

How far are teachers conscious of these differences in perception? The main report describes a case study of a male teacher who taught two parallel but single sex groups - one male, one female. The groups clearly saw both their classroom experience and the teacher differently. While the teacher conceded that there were some differences in his approach to the groups, his responses failed to pick up either the number of items on which the groups perceived him differently or the degree of significant difference.

One is left to ponder on the extent to which the differences in student perception, and the behavioural adjustments of the teacher, both acknowledged and unacknowledged, are indeed gender-related and the scope for increased effectiveness in the learning of both sexes if levels of teacher consciousness about student perceptions were higher. Adjustment in teaching strategies might then become conscious and planned.

Students by ethnic origin

It had been the intention of the project to examine the perceptions of students from a range of ethnic backgrounds, and a number of inner city schools/colleges were accordingly included in the sample. However, although a wide variety of ethnic backgrounds is represented in the sample only two groups were of sufficient size to merit statistical analysis. These were students who classified themselves as being of UK/Irish or Asian (Indian subcontinent) ethnic origin. The latter included students from families that had been formerly resident in East Africa. The two groups constituted approximately seventy nine per cent and seventeen per cent respectively of the student sample. Asian students were found in forty two per cent of the classes studied and their representation in physics was double that in history groups.

Significant difference in perception existed in respect of seven strategy and nine characteristic variables. One strong feature of the Asian student response is that these students express a considerably lower level of active involvement in class than their UK/Irish peers. They consider that there is a lower frequency of students asking questions, student presentations and class discussion than UK/Irish students perceive. They also by comparison see their teachers less as someone who encourages students to express their own ideas.

The fact that these students feel that their teachers talk to them significantly less frequently on their own level than do students of UK/Irish origin suggests that language may be a contributory inhibitor to active involvement. If this is the case then this is highly disturbing. It may equally be true that the expression of lower levels of active involvement should be considered in relation to lower indicators of their recourse to teachers. Asian students clearly view their teachers as less significant to the totality of their subject learning than do UK/Irish students, with the teacher seen less as a source of information, guidance and encouragement. If this is correct we might look perhaps to cultural explanations.This section, like those above, is concerned to establish that students from identifiable subpopulations collectively appear to perceive class-room reality differently from students from other groups. While it is hoped that these results will cast some light on the phenomenon, raise awareness and encourage teachers working in a multiethnic environment to pose questions about the differential effects of their pedagogy, it is important to stress that this is all that is attempted; no claims are made to an understanding of the complex interactions of linguistic, cultural and other factors which interact with the students' A-level subject learning.

CONCLUSION

The empirical research described above supports the findings of recent HMI surveys on the classroom experience of A-level students. However, it goes further in raising questions about the present status of A-level classroom process in professional discussion between colleagues and, more ominously, in the consciousness of individual teachers who appear singularly unable to describe with precision their repertoire of strategies, or the incidence of particular strategies which they use to transact A-level curricula in their classrooms.

It is our contention that A-level pedagogy is an acutely urgent issue for schools and colleges to address, although the task before institutional managers is not underestimated. However, it is our belief that the rewards are great. A-level pedagogy is the key to significant change in the sixteen to nineteen curriculum. It has the potency to permit august whole-school aims to be met and to enable the potential of more students, in respect of an ever-increasing range of aspirations, to be realised.

Acknowledgement

The writer would like to acknowledge the contribution of Rob Johnson who jointly undertook the research described in this chapter.

References

DES (1988) *Advancing A-levels* : The Report of the Higginson Committee, para 2.13 p. 7.

HMI (1984) Report by HM Inspectors on St Philip's Sixth Form College, Birmingham (Roman Catholic, voluntary aided) para 23.6 p. 34, para 12.11 p. 20

HMI (1988a) *A Survey of Sixth Form Colleges in England*, para 24, p.8; paras 20, 21 p.7. HMI, London.

HMI (1988b) *Secondary Schools: An Appraisal by HMI*, para 111, p.29. HMI, London.

HMI (1986) *A Survey of the Teaching of A Level English Literature in 20 'Mixed' Sixth Forms in Comprehensive Schools*, para 3.3, p.9. HMI, London.

The Leicestershire LEA Curriculum Statement: Draft Working Document (1988), December, para 25-26 p.5, LEA, Leicestershire.

Mayne P.W. (1986) *Perceptions of teaching strategies in the A-level classroom*, unpublished MEd dissertation, Leicester University School of Education.

Mayne P.W. (1988) *Teaching and learning styles in the A-level classroom: departmental awareness, discussion and policy making*, unpublished paper.

Mitchell, Peter (1987) *The Post-16 Curriculum - A Discussion Paper*, mimeo, Leicestershire Education Department.

Pam, S. (1984) History teaching in the sixth form, in *Teaching History*, No 39

Simon B. (1981) 'Why no pedagogy in England?', in Simon, B. and Taylor, W. (eds) *Education in the Eighties: the central issues*. Batsford Academic and Educational Ltd, London.

Suddaby, Adam (1989) *The 16-19 Curriculum - A Discussion Paper*, para 4.21, pp.31-32. Warwickshire Education Department

Times Educational Supplement (1989) Universities attack sixth form history: Exeter survey reveals that very few professors are happy with A-levels, 9 June.

Chapter 8

Effective learning and the critical thinking movement

Alec Fisher

Like many other teachers, Ernest wanted to teach his pupils to *reason* well, to eschew bad arguments and to value good ones, to be *clear-headed*, and to *think for themselves*. Ernest wanted his pupils to learn these skills and values in his own field, but he also hoped that they would *transfer* to other subjects.

Over the years, Ernest came to feel that his hopes were not being realised and that he was failing to teach *general and transferable thinking skills*. (At the very best, there was no *evidence* that he was succeeding in this). After discussing the problem with colleagues, he discovered that many experiments in teaching transferable thinking skills were taking place, and that experimental materials were available to help him. That was how Ernest became involved in the 'critical thinking movement'.

THE ORIGINS OF THE CRITICAL THINKING MOVEMENT

Although teachers have been interested in teaching people to think at least since Socrates, current concerns with critical thinking are generally traced back to the work of the American philosopher, psychologist and educationist, John Dewey. One of the first discussions of critical thinking - which Dewey called 'reflective thinking' - is to be found in his book *How We Think* (1909), based on his work in the Chicago Laboratory School, and much of it reflects conversations with teachers who were trying to implement his ideas. An important and striking feature of the book is the extent to which it is interdisciplinary - it draws on philosophy, on psychology and on teaching experience - and that is very characteristic of modern work on critical thinking.

The next major development in the critical thinking tradition was probably Edward Glaser's *An Experiment in the Development of Critical Thinking*, published in 1941. While he was a student at the Advanced School of Education at Teacher's College, Columbia University, Glaser designed an experiment into the teaching of critical thinking which was a model of scientific method. His

An earlier version of this paper was published in Coles, M. J. and Robinson, W. D. (eds), (1989) *Teaching Thinking*, Bristol Press and is reproduced here by permission.

procedure was as follows. He devised a range of teaching materials for the use of teachers in teaching critical thinking. The teachers were then briefed on the objectives of the experiment and on the basic concepts and methods involved. After the teachers had each taught a ten week course in critical thinking, their students' critical thinking abilities were assessed and compared with the abilities of children in control groups who had had no special instruction.

The *Watson-Glaser critical thinking appraisal* was developed as part of this study and, since its initial development, revised versions of this test have been widely used to test critical thinking abilities. It is now probably the most widely used test of critical thinking abilities in the world (despite its manifest weaknesses).

Though it seems unlikely to us now that a ten week course could have any lasting effect on critical thinking abilities, Glaser's pioneering study is of considerable historical importance in the development of the critical thinking tradition.

In 1962 the *Harvard Education Review* published an article by Robert Ennis which is still rightly regarded as a landmark in this field. The article was called 'A concept of critical thinking: a proposed basis for research in the teaching and evaluation of critical thinking ability' and its objective was to detail what critical thinking means and entails.

In this article, Ennis breaks 'critical thinking' into its constituent parts. These include grasping the *meaning* of a statement, avoiding *ambiguity*, spotting *contradictions*, judging what *follows*, what is *assumed* and when a conclusion is *warranted*, deciding when a *definition* is adequate, when an *observation statement* or *authority* are reliable, and deciding when a problem has been properly *identified* and adequately resolved. Ennis also presents a detailed discussion of each of the elements he has identified, which is intended to be sufficient for teaching and evaluation purposes.

Much of this early work was conducted in relative isolation. However, the past two decades have seen a rapid growth in what has become known as the 'informal logic and critical thinking' movement. This is not so much a 'movement' as a large number of related experiments. These experiments differ in many ways but they all share a similar objective; this is to improve reasoning skills and critical thinking skills by *direct* methods - that is, methods designed specifically for that purpose.

In part these experiments have arisen as a reaction against the belief that reasoning skills are best taught *indirectly* - in other words, by teaching some other *subject* such as elementary formal logic, classics, history or mathematics. The problem with the indirect approach is that *transfer* simply does not occur. In part these experiments have arisen as a reaction against the belief that all reasoning is subject-specific. On this view the only way to learn to reason well in a given field is to master the subject matter of that field, say, history, physics, medicine or whatever. (For a forceful exposition of this view see John McPeck's (1981) *Critical Thinking and Education*, which is discussed below.) The problem with this view is that it claims too much. An *ad hominem* fallacy is a fallacy in any field. More generally, there are principles of reasoning which apply in many fields. However, the main drive behind these various experiments appears to be an increasing demand for general reasoning skills and a widespread conviction that clear and logical thinking ought to be teachable.

SOME CURRENT PROGRAMMES

In this section we briefly explain three current approaches to teaching critical thinking, which belong in the informal logic and critical thinking tradition.

Informal logic

Informal logic courses are mostly aimed at the college and university level. In these, students are taught at the very least how to identify the conclusions, reasons and structure of a piece of reasoning. This is usually done by using linguistic clues. Students are then given some general criteria for distinguishing good and bad arguments; these sometimes include some standard propositional logic, some classic fallacies and the deductive-inductive distinction and sometimes not. The key point is that the method concentrates on real arguments, taken from sources ranging from newspapers to classic texts, rather than on the usual, invented ones, familiar to formal logicians. Michael Scriven's (1976) book *Reasoning* set the agenda for this kind of approach. One of the most widely used textbooks in this tradition is Trudy Govier's (1985) *A Practical Study of Argument*.

The philosophy for children programme

The philosophy for children programme is the creation of Matthew Lipman, formerly Professor of Philosophy at Columbia University before he established the Institute for the Advancement of Philosophy for Children (IAPC) at Montclair State College, New York.

Lipman's explicit objective was to teach children to *think* for themselves instead of learning by rote and simply accepting the authority of their teachers. It is easy to have this laudable aim but it is much harder to devise a curriculum that will realise it. His main interest is in developing reasoning skills so that children can 'draw sound inferences, offer convincing reasons, flush out underlying assumptions, establish defensible classifications and definitions, organise coherent explanations, descriptions and arguments' (Lipman, 1985); and he can now cite good empirical evidence that his programme is successful and that children taught reasoning through philosophy have shown marked improvement in reasoning skills (Lipman and Gazzard, 1989).

Lipman's method is to train school teachers to use his specially prepared material - notably the novels *Harry Stottlemeier's Discovery* (Lipman 1974) and *Lisa* (Lipman, 1976) - the teachers then return to their schools to teach reasoning skills. Whatever the age of the children the procedure is roughly similar: the children read an episode from one of the novels and choose what they want to talk about. The characters in the novel are themselves children who are modelling what Lipman wants his readers to do - that is, reasoning, defining, explaining, trying to deal with ambiguity, etc. Lipman claims that children quickly identify with the characters in the novel and learn to play the same game. The teacher is provided with a manual that describes numerous possible lesson plans but is not meant to impose his or her answers.

A brief example will give the flavour of Lipman's approach. In one episode, a child is nearly hit by a stone. He immediately assumes that the stone was deliberately thrown at him by someone. In subsequent discussion of this episode children sometimes point out that such an assumption is not necessarily appropriate, and this is then the cue for the teacher to introduce an exercise in assumption-hunting - the teacher being supplied with instructive examples in the teacher's manual.

Lipman claims (1985) that : 'In time, the students begin to develop a commendable wariness, a critical disposition which will be invaluable to them in their encounters with other academic disciplines if they are given the opportunity to discuss the epistemological conditions under which factual claims are made'.

The Institute for the Advancement of Philosophy for Children now has centres in many parts of the world, especially in Europe and in North and South America. Its growth in recent years has been quite remarkable. Of course Lipman's programme has its critics. Some say that good teachers have always done such things. Some teachers who have used his techniques say that they need a deeper philosophical training to be successful. Others say that *transfer* does not take place from one subject to another. However, this is a very interesting experiment which surely deserves more serious study in the United Kingdom.

'Strong' critical thinking

In another notable experiment, students are not only taught the 'microskills' of the informal logician, but they are also taught (where appropriate) to locate arguments in a broader cultural context, to recognise their personal prejudices and the prejudices of their society, and they are shown how to evaluate arguments in this broader context. The leading exponent of this approach is Professor Richard Paul, Director of the Centre for Critical Thinking and Moral Critique at Sonoma State University, California. As he puts it in a recent paper 'Critical thinking and the critical person' (Paul, 1989):

'Much that we learn ... is distinctly irrational. [We] come to believe any number of things without knowing how or why ... [We] believe for irrational reasons: because those around us believe, because we are rewarded for believing, because we are afraid to disbelieve, because our vested interest is served by belief... In all of these cases our beliefs are without rational grounding ... we become rational on the other hand, to the extent that our beliefs and actions are grounded in good reasons and evidence ... to the extent we have cultivated a passion for clarity, accuracy and fairmindedness. These global skills, passions and dispositions, integrated with a way of acting and thinking are what characterise the rational, the educated and, in my sense, the critical person.'

Another source of materials for those who wish to experiment with teaching critical thinking is to be found in a series of books by Professor Paul. The main purpose of each book is to help school teachers to remodel their lessons so that they teach critical thinking skills (in short, exactly what Ernest was looking for). The first book in the series is called *Critical Thinking Handbook. K-3: A Guide for Remodelling Lesson Plans in Language, Arts, Social Studies and Science* (Paul, Binker and Charbonneau, 1986). It is aimed at those teaching children in the range kindergarten to grade three (children aged five to eight); the second is for grades four to six (children aged nine to eleven). A third, for grades six to nine, is just published, and a fourth, for 'high school' students, is due out shortly. (In what follows we shall refer to the first book as *K-3* and the second as *4-6*; Paul *et al.*, 1987).

Each book is self-contained and each has the same form. First, there is a general account of what critical thinking is, and then there is an explanatory list of 'strategies' for teaching critical thinking (twenty eight strategies in *K-3*; thirty one in *4-6*). However, most of the book comprises lesson plans in their original and remodelled forms. The originals are criticised in the light of the principles of critical thinking, and the reasons for the remodelled plans are explained in terms of the strategies for teaching critical thinking (fifty eight lessons in *K-3*; forty in *4-6*).

Two brief examples, from *K-3*, will give the flavour. In the first (p. 183) the issue is whether air has weight. In the original lesson plan, children learn that air has weight by doing two experiments. In one they balance two full balloons on a yardstick and then let the air out of one of the balloons. In the other experiment they compare the weight of a basketball when it is empty and when it is full of air.

In the revised lesson plan, the teacher begins with the question 'Does air weigh anything?' and allows discussion. The next question is, 'How could we find out?' Here, the objective is to 'foster independent thinking' (strategy one). The children may need to be led to think of the experiments just mentioned or something similar, but the intention is to get the children to do as much as possible themselves. When they have done the experiments (or any others they thought of) they are asked, 'What did you observe? What did you conclude? How did the experiment settle the issue?' and the objective is to get the children to explain their reasoning as fully as possible (strategy eighteen) and to make them 'comfortable' about doing this and being expected to do it. Part of this process requires them to make their assumptions explicit (strategy fourteen), and the teacher encourages this with suitable questioning.

So much for a scientific example. Other examples illustrate even better what is distinctive about Paul's work. Paul is best known for his distinction between 'weak' and 'strong' critical thinking. In short, the weak critical thinker is skilled in the techniques of argument, but uses these skills only to pursue his or her own narrow selfish interests. The strong critical thinker is skilled in the techniques of argument, and uses them 'fairmindedly'. Fairminded critical thinkers not only subject the views of other people and other societies (having interests and ideologies different from their own) to critical scrutiny, but they are just as ready to subject their own interests, preferences, prejudices and ideologies to critical scrutiny.

A very brief example from *K-3* (p. 83) should illustrate the idea. In this lesson the children read a story. In the story Eddie collects things that he calls 'valuable property', but which his father calls 'junk'. One day Eddie buys two objects from an antique shop. At first his father is angry, but then he decided he wants one of the objects and he buys it from Eddie. Eddie's mother buys the other. Eddie's father is proud of the profit Eddie made and suggests they go into business together 'selling junk'.

In the original lesson plan, pupils are asked to do the following things: recall story details; guess Eddie's mother's attitude; list objects found in the antique shops; make and justify inferences; describe the difference between junk and antiques; calculate Eddie's profit; and select a sentence that expresses the main idea of the story.

In his critique of this lesson plan Paul says:

'This story describes a clash of two perspectives. The disagreement between Eddie and his father provides an excellent model for many conflicts. It includes a specific issue (that is, 'Does Eddie collect junk or valuable property?'); two sets of incompatible concepts applied to the same phenomena; and two lines of reasoning based on contradictory evaluative assumptions (i.e., objects which look interesting or appealing are valuable; only those objects which can be used or sold for profit are valuable). Yet the suggested questions fail to take advantage of the story' (*K-3* p. 83).

In the remodelled lesson plan, children are asked to *identify key concepts* themselves - rather than being told them - thus *fostering independent thinking* (strategy one). They are asked to *clarify these concepts* with examples (strategy twelve), and to say what is *implied* by calling something 'junk', etc. (strategy twenty one). They are also asked to *identify the assumptions held* by Eddie and his father, including their different values (strategy fourteen), and to try to *see things from both perspectives* (strategy three). They are also asked to carefully note the facts in the case, to distinguish those that are *relevant* from those that are *irrelevant* to the argument (strategy sixteen) and to distinguish the facts from what they (the pupils) *infer* from them (strategy seventeen). They are also asked to say what changed through the story 'Was it assumptions, use of terms, values, or what?' They may also engage in dialogue and role-playing, etc.

The emphasis throughout is on getting children to think for themselves. The objective is that they should be clearheaded and should reason through things for themselves, especially by considering alternative perspectives, *and that they should value doing this*. The method employed by the teacher is essentially that of Socratic questioning and dialogue, 'What does this *mean*? What is Eddie *assuming*? What is *implied*?', etc.

Paul's books are written for North American children, so that the examples and style do not always readily transfer to the British context. However, this too is an experiment from which we may learn, and Paul has plans to produce a handbook for the British market in the near future.

JOHN McPECK'S CHALLENGE

The most notable and systematic critique of the critical thinking tradition whose emergence we have been describing, is to be found in John McPeck's (1981) book *Critical Thinking and Education*. His position is clearly expressed in the following paragraph:

> '[critical thinking] is the appropriate use of *reflective scepticism* within the problem area under consideration, and knowing how and when to apply this reflective scepticism effectively requires, among other things, knowing something about the field in question. Thus we may say of someone that he is a critical thinker about X if he has the propensity and skill to engage in X (be it mathematics, politics or mountain climbing) with reflective scepticism. There is, moreover, no reason to believe that a person who thinks critically in one area will be able to do so in another. The transfer of training skills cannot be assumed of critical thinking but must be established in each case by means of empirical tests. Calling to witness such notorious cases as distinguished logicians with no idea for whom to vote, nor why, it is fair to postulate that no one can think critically about everything, as there are no Renaissance men in this age of specialised knowledge' (p. 7).

In short, McPeck's view is that critical thinking is *subject-specific*, that what *counts* as critical thinking differs from subject to subject, that there are no *general* skills which can be applied in all fields, and that therefore there is no reason to expect *transfer* of critical thinking skills from one domain to another (that is, one could be a critical thinker in one field without being anything of the sort in others).

McPeck's criticisms have generated many strong reactions from those working in the field in North America. In Britain, they appear to accord well with current opinion.

References

Dewey, J. (1909) *How We Think*, D. C. Heath and Co., Boston

Ennis, R. H. (1962) A concept of critical thinking, *Harvard Educational Review*, (32), 1, pp. 81-111.

Ennis, R. H. and Norris, S. (1989) *Evaluating Critical Thinking*, Midwest Publications, Pacific Grove, CA

Ennis, R. H. (1981) Rational thinking and educational practice, in J. Soltis (ed.) *Philosophy and Education*, Vol. 1 of the eightieth yearbook of the National Society for the Study of Education, NSSE, Chicago.

Fisher, A. E. (ed.) (1988) *Critical Thinking: Proceedings of the First British Conference on Informal Logic and Critical Thinking*, University of East Anglia.

Glaser, E. (1941) *An Experiment in the Development of Critical Thinking*, Teachers College, Colombia University, New York .

Govier, T. (1985) *A Practical Study of Argument*, Wadsworth Publishing Co., Belmont CA.

Lipman, M. (1974) *Harry Stottlemeier's Discovery*, Institute for the Advancement of Philosophy for Children, Montelair, NJ.

Lipman, M. (1976) *Lisa*, Institute for the Advancement of Philosophy for Children, Montelair, NJ.

Lipman, M. and Gazzard, A. (1989) *Philosophy for Children: Where We Are Now ...*, Supplement Two, Institute for the Advancement of Philosophy for Children, Montelair, NJ.

Lipman, M. (1985) Philosophy for children and critical thinking, *National Forum*, Winter pp. 18-21.

McPeck, J. (1981) *Critical Thinking and Education*, Robertson, Oxford.

Paul, R., Binker, A. J. A. and Charbonneau, M. (1986) *Critical Thinking Handbook K-3*, Center for Critical Thinking and Moral Critique, Sonoma State University, CA

Paul, R., Binker, A. J. A., Martin, D. and Adamson, K. (1989) *Critical Thinking Handbook: High School*, Center for Critical Thinking and Moral Critique, Sonoma State University, CA.

Paul, R. *et al* (1987) *Critical Thinking Handbook 4-6*, Centre for Critical Thinking and Moral Critique, Sonoma State University, Washington.

Paul, R. (1989) Critical thinking and the critical person in Perkins, D. (ed) (1989), *Thinking: Progress in Research and Teaching,* Bishop and Lockhead. Lawrence Erlbaum Associates Inc, Hillside, NJ.

Paul, R. (1985) The critical thinking movement, *National Forum*, Winter, 1985, pp. 2-3.

Scriven, M. (1976) *Reasoning*, McGraw-Hill, New York

Part III

MONITORING AND ACCOUNTABILITY
Evaluating effective learning

Introduction

'It is tempting to argue that accountability in the system must have *one* purpose. Yet, if there are a variety of parties on either side of an accountability relation they may interpret that purpose differently and have additional purposes of their own' (Sockett, 1982).

Two apparently conflicting forces are present in the current growth of monitoring and accountability. First, the wider political environment within which education operates at the close of the 1980s and into the 1990s, and out of which grew ERA, is conditioned by the use of the overpowering metaphor of the market place. The language in which education is discussed is that of manufacturing industry and commerce, and this is seen most clearly in endeavours to evaluate its 'process' and 'product' against measures of efficiency, effectiveness and value for money. However, this coexists, second, with a force originating in the profession itself to monitor work in individual classrooms and schools in a more systematic and sophisticated way, to use this process to improve the learning of children and to communicate quality and effectiveness to those outside the school.

The contributors to this section explore a range of avenues in the evaluation of effective learning in schools and colleges, and on the impact of demands for greater accountability in the system, both in the United Kingdom and the United States. While each brings a particular focus and context to the discussion of these issues, they are united in their belief that external pressures for accountability can be harnessed for the benefit of the learning of children in our classrooms.

Fashions in issues of accountability are subject to the rhythms of societal, political and economic change and as such lack permanence - this time round! Hence there is a critical professional role for teachers in determining measures of effectiveness which can be owned as supporting effective learning in their classrooms and which, as Professor Kysilka says, possess 'the characteristic of timelessness, for who knows what tomorrow brings?' The external demand can thus be translated sensitively into the internal growth of an evaluative culture in classrooms and schools which both maximises the opportunities for effective learning and allows teachers to develop professionally.

Professor Davis opens with the question 'Who is the curriculum customer?'. In this chapter he rejects the well-worn metaphors of 'the garden' or 'the factory', and argues instead that we should see education in terms of the 'market place'. Using this metaphor the curriculum is neither the means by which pupils are helped to blossom through the cultivation of their talents nor the process by which they are received, transformed, delivered or produced. Rather the curriculum is the merchandise offered by the school, the teachers the sales staff and the pupils the customers who pay with their time, talents and energy for the curriculum offering they elect to buy. This revision of metaphor in conceptualising education is an interesting starting point for considering monitoring and accountability.

The concept of the teacher's accountability to the pupil is central to Sheirer's paper. In the United Kingdom and the United States those professionally engaged in education are concerned by the threat of the 'deprofessionalisation' of teaching. The latter is seen in the way in which educational decision-making occurs less and less in the classroom and in schools, but involves government agencies more and more. At the same time public concerns that all students in the state system attain certain levels of competence, regardless of which school they attend, foster demands for increased accountability of teachers. Hence schools are in receipt of demands for bureaucratic statements of objectives and under populist pressure to return to a golden age when teachers taught and students learnt! Both suppose learning to be a far more simplistic process than in reality it is.

The chapter explores the perceived lack of congruence between the demand for accountability and the teacher's professional responsibility to represent knowledge to children in ways that promote learning. In its focus on the teacher's role the paper outlines an active response to bridge these concerns. The teacher thus relates the demands of knowledge acquisition to the child in such a way as to make learning both personally meaningful and sociologically and politically accountable. The rationale for the work of teachers is plain. 'We need not be in conflict,' says Sheirer 'with those who worry with us about children's learning.'

The 1980s have witnessed a series of major shifts in approaches to student assessment, recording and reporting in the United Kingdom. This has been seen in the 'profiling' and records of achievement movement - essentially grassroot and classroom based - the 'GCSE revolution', the TGAT Report and, even more powerfully, in the statutory arrangements for assessing, recording and reporting achievement in the National Curriculum. As we enter the 1990s a great deal relating to the latter and its relationship to other strands of assessment and recording still has to be clarified and understood. While, as Munby observes, this 'situation ... remains one of uncertainty and shifting ground' there are already signs of further major shifts elsewhere on the educational horizon as the Secretary of State assumes certain of his reserve powers in respect of the sixteen to nineteen curriculum.

Stephen Munby's chapter continues the theme of the teacher's accountability to the student within the British context of records of achievement process and the 1988 Education Act. He articulates a powerful rationale for records of achievement as a means of enhancing effective learning, and notes the findings of the PRAISE Report that a continuing consensus exists 'that records of achievement can raise the standard of pupils' learning by raising their involvement in, their commitment to, and their enjoyment of, the educational process' (PRAISE team, 1988).

It is unfortunate that much professional discussion on records of achievement has been limited to the summative document. This has often missed the point and left records of achievement peculiarly vulnerable, as witnessed by the events of August 1989, 'the month that records of achievement died' (Munby, 1989). Whatever uncertainty may exist currently on the status of summative documents, Munby demonstrates the nature of formative records of achievement process as sound classroom process *per se* by reference to six fundamental learning principles. In exploring assessment, recording and reporting issues in the post-ERA environment he exhorts local education authorities, school senior management and classroom teachers to be proactive and not merely to wait supinely for the letter of statutory orders to emerge. To do the latter would be to adopt a minimalist stance content to provide 'glorified reports containing mainly numbers and levels'. These have little to do with effective learning and formative assessing and recording of children's achievement in classrooms. Instead he argues for local education authorities and schools to adopt coherent assessment policies. He writes, 'there is nothing in the Education Reform Act to prevent LEAs, schools and teachers from implementing the six learning principles ... within and beyond the National Curriculum.'

Ultimately effective learning is determined by what is measured according to the demands of society. Hence if society demands 'product', and schools teach and assess 'product', effective learning may be said to have occurred. The problem is that demand changes and often reactively. In a paper that allows for considerable parallels with issues in the post-ERA environment in the United Kingdom, Professor Kysilka traces the ebb and flow of the process-product debate in the United States. She highlights the way in which the demands of public opinion and changing work force requirements can easily go out of synchronisation. Public opinion which imposed the 'shackles' of a 'back to basics' approach failed to foresee the way in which higher order skills were being underdeveloped until too late. Hence like Scheirer, she argues a special place for the teacher in tempering the extremes by maintaining a balanced and effective curriculum which will equip young people for life roles in a changing world, irrespective of the vicissitudes of public opinion. She warns that any approach to learning - however good - is liable to be stigmatised as ineffective if it is assessed by inappropriate instruments designed to test other objectives. Effective learning can only be guaranteed where classroom process, methods of student assessment and teacher professional development are kept in harmony with the development of curricular objectives.

Increasing emphasis in the United Kingdom on value for money, school accountability, teacher appraisal and parental choice has led to a surge of interest in approaches to the assessment of school performance. Early work in this field has led to the development of quantitative performance indicators that focus exclusively on outcome and barely impact on the work of classroom teachers and the learning of children. By contrast Skilling and Sutton argue that the raising of standards and improvements in the quality of student experience depend on the professional skills of teachers. It is therefore essential that the teacher is fully involved in the development of any measures of student performance. The authors have been working on the practical realisation of this with sixty five school and seven college TVEI coordinators in Leicestershire. Their model seeks to develop performance targets and indicators that relate to process as well as outcome and are qualitative in dimension. As with the other papers in this section the student is at the very heart of the process and the classroom teacher crucially involved in evaluation as part of curriculum and professional development.

References

Munby, S. (1989) The month records of achievement died, *Times Educational Supplement*, 29 September.

PRAISE Team (1988) *Records of Achievement, Report of the National Evaluation of Pilot Schemes*, HMSO, London.

Sockett, H. (1982) Accountability: purpose and meaning, in McCormick, R. (ed.) *Calling Education to Account*, Heinemann, London.

Chapter 9

Who is the curriculum customer?

O L Davis Jr.

One critical question drives decisions of a business enterprise in a market economy. Among other important questions, its centrality is crucial to successful businesses. It is compelling. Inattentive responses foreshadow business failure.

'Who is the customer?'

The question's saliency remains undiminished regardless of the nature of business - businesses of service, businesses of products. 'Who is the customer?' demands as much attention in the mature organisation as it does in the initial steps of a business plan for a fledgling enterprise.

In these days, when the metaphor of the market dominates so much of the rhetoric of education, a surprising silence, much like a dense fog, hangs over debate about educational policies and programmes. It is a silence born of an unvoiced question, 'Who is the customer?' The silence is particularly intense in matters concerning the school curriculum. Specifically, the question, 'Who is the customer for the curriculum?' is never uttered. Implicit in a few proposals and responses, to be sure, have been feebly formed and mainly ambiguous notions of 'customer' for the curriculum. Perhaps one reason for this impressive silence is that the answer to the unvoiced questions appears to be self-evident. Or, maybe, it is perceived to be trivial.

The question of customer is central to every consideration of each enterprise operating in a market economy. Indeed, this question assumes more profound significance to schooling and the curriculum - when they are set within the metaphor of the market - precisely because consideration of this question has been so fundamentally and continuously ignored. To allege that the market is an inappropriate metaphor for schooling is an arguable point. I presently believe, however, that such disputation is only personally decorative and publicly alienating. For us educationists to persist in such display is for us not to be taken seriously by politicians and opinion moulders, nor by the general citizenry. It is also for us to opt out of the thoughtful invention of education's future. Simply, we must join the larger society's efforts to reform education and, for some of our time, we must employ the metaphor of the market clearly dominant in public discourse. I suggest that our initial step be to pose - and help answer - the great market question in education, 'Who is the curriculum customer?' This essay constitutes a first effort in this regard.

We must acknowledge a handicap in our and society's consideration of this question. In so doing, we may well come to know a strange liberation of mind. The handicap we have is simply recognised because it has two principal attributes. Most of us find the question, at least at the outset, so very unusual and strange that it is all but obscene. 'Customers' for the curriculum? The term 'customer' is alien to every conventional curriculum construct.

We are accustomed to metaphors of a different sort in our preferred manners of thinking about curriculum and schooling. One comfortable metaphor, of course, is that of the garden. Business provides another, but is not as satisfying. Indeed, it is not a full-bodied and robust metaphor of business but, rather, one related only to a specific dimension of business: manufacturing. Its code word, 'factory', has fuelled much thinking about education throughout this century. Inputs and products partake of this manufacturing metaphor, as do processes and delivery. So, also, do standards and accountability and costs and resources and schedules. My question 'Who is the curriculum customer?' offends precisely because neither gardens nor factories have customers. Moreover, manufacturing has commonly been perceived as encompassing all of business. This perception is a key error and two simple facts are correctives. All business in a market economy is not dependent on manufacturing. No business enterprise can exist without customers.

So, who is the curriculum customer?

Instantly, the question reconceptualises the school. Many former images simply collapse like spent balloons. In this new question, the school does not produce anything. No 'raw materials' are carted to the school to be moulded or shaped or installed. No 'parts' are riveted or welded or glued or wired to others. No ingredient is mixed with another substance, heated or cooled, baked or painted. The previously popular images from manufacturing - the industrial factory - are seen to be empty and dry. Consequently, they must be abandoned. The school, through this question, must be re-seen and freshly known: it is a venue for sales. At school, something is offered for sale. There, persons - as customers - buy or do not buy what is offered for sale. Furthermore, that offered for sale is either taken - bought - or is refused to remain 'on the shelf' as dusty inventory.

The curriculum also is reconceptualised by the insistent market question. The curriculum does not act on anyone. It does not shape or mould or create or change anyone. It is not a process by which individuals are received, transformed, delivered, or produced. These are functions of manufacturing, and the insistent question about customer identity evaporates their claims to meaning about the curriculum. In the renewed context of the market-place question, the curriculum regains its birthright. Simply, the curriculum must be known as the offering of the school. As certainly, the curriculum is not the 'taking' by anyone; 'taking' constitutes the actions of individuals who buy what is offered. The curriculum is what is available for customers to buy ... or to choose not to buy.

But who is the curriculum customer? Only one responsible answer to this simple question is possible.

Pupils are the curriculum customers.

As customers, pupils act; they are not acted upon. They are not pawns to be moved or shifted according to some elegant or brutish strategy. Certainly, they are not 'raw material' to be manipulated by 'processes' any more than they are not 'vessels' to be filled. As customers, pupils choose to buy ... and not to buy. This simple truth, rephrased in the conventional language of education, has long been known, but, also, has been long obscured by that same language: pupils learn ... and do not learn. Pupils decide what of the offering (curriculum) they will take away with them. They select which elements of the offering, in history, for example - the Punic Wars, the names of Italian kingdoms, the causes of the American Civil War, the successes and failures of the Lyndon Johnson presidency - they will buy ... or take away ... or learn ... or not.

Pupils, acting as customers, buy as they act to learn. They 'pay' their time and talents and energy for the curriculum offering they select. Properly, in market meanings, their purchase must be separated conceptually from their acts, their engagements, their considerations prior to purchase.

To be sure, some of the curriculum pupils buy is learned. Some is learned and remembered over a long period, even a lifetime. We all know examples. Benedict Arnold, an American traitor, Elizabeth Barrett Browning's evocative poetic images, the Pythagorean theorem. Both facts and concepts. Both ways of thinking and sentiments. On the other hand, some of the curriculum bought is known to possess only temporal value and is abandoned quickly - soon after a test, for example, learned only for a short time and for a narrowly defined purpose. And some of the curriculum is simply not bought, and, consequently, not learned for a host of reasons, some of them particular to individual customers, some because of interest and use ('I'm not interested in any Danish prince, even if his name is Hamlet.' 'I guess I couldn't realise then that I would ever need to understand what a "profit and loss statement" is'). Some is not bought because of the offering itself. (The material (content) is inappropriate for the age or state of prior knowledge of the pupil/customer, for example). Other offerings are not purchased because of pupils' reactions to the 'display', 'packaging', 'timing', 'presentation', or 'engagement with' the curriculum/offering. All of us recognise that some offerings are not bought for reasons having to do with the particular salesperson 'showing' the curriculum element ('I just can't abide Mrs Elzner', and 'I would like anything Mr Maxwell taught').

Some pupils, as customers, exhibit 'resistance' to the curriculum which is offered to them. They may do nothing with the offering (for example, inattention in class sessions, failure to complete assignments). They may appear to be underachieving. That is, these pupils/customers make only a modest effort to buy the curriculum/offering, just enough at times, when important to them, for example, to escape the wrath of parents. Pupils also decide to leave school. These 'dropouts' decide that the school's offerings are not valuable enough for them to choose or, that the opportunity costs of the offering are simply too exorbitant and they would rather spend their time and talents elsewhere (for example, in the workplace) and for which they receive money rather than tokens (for example, grades) in exchange for their expenditures.

In each of the circumstances mentioned here too briefly, the idea of pupils as customers of the curriculum enlivens educational thought and action. It transforms the image of school beyond a kind of 'palace of civic virtue' or a 'physics-factory', as two examples, to notions of the school as market, trades fair, bazaar, supermarket, a group of boutiques, or mall. As well, a bright market spotlight is focused on the insufficiency of current educational practices and organisation to accommodate most pupils (customers). Absolutely necessary would be renewed attention to the very nature of the curriculum's (offerings) richness, variety, robustness, and attractiveness, even its/their usefulness.

We recognise immediately, in this kind of conception, that, while pupils are properly the curriculum customers, other individuals and groups are not customers of the schools' offerings. Future employers of pupils certainly are not curriculum customers. In all likelihood, parents, as well, are not curriculum customers - even if they assert that they are. And neither is the citizenry at large. Rather, pupils as curriculum customers make possible a more fruitful conception, in market terms, of the roles of parents and other adults.

The general public appropriately might be understood as shareholders in the public schooling enterprise. Within this very large group of shareholders, parents might well constitute a special class of shareholders whose special warrants continue only during the tenure of their children in particular schools. Shareholders express their concerns and interests about both the general schooling enterprise and particular school operations. They also select boards of trustees and governors to make and oversee policies in the interest of all the shareholders/citizens. Clearly, both short-term and long-term interests and purposes are the province of these shareholder-directors. Shareholders clearly are not 'patrons'. And, as certainly, they are not curriculum customers.

Understanding pupils as customers of the curriculum requires other reconceptualisations, as well. Teachers cannot be known as 'deliverers' or 'guides' or 'directors'. The concept of customer requires that teaching be reseen as the process by which the curriculum (offering) is made available and desirable to customers (pupils). Both for a 'poor curriculum' (for example, limited, restricted, impoverished offerings) and for a 'rich curriculum' (for example, many options, many robust meanings and instructional materials, varied environments for study), teaching as 'presentation' on a 'take-it-or-leave-it' basis ignores the concept of pupils as curriculum customers.

Also, the nature of school administration, leadership and management, must also be refashioned for consistency with pupils as curriculum customers. School principals, for example, might well act analogously to 'store managers' whose routines relate to motivation and continuing education of teachers, to working with teachers to help develop new, fresh approaches to the active engagement of pupils/customers with the goods and services (offerings) available in the school, and to increasing the general attractiveness of the school as an institution and of the engagements (for example, shopping, looking, examining, 'trying-on', resting, wandering, purchasing) possible with teachers and pupils.

Who is the curriculum customer? is a simple business question. Its response, on the other hand, looses a torrent of possible meanings and wonderment. Those suggested here constitute but a sample of the rich possibilities. Certainly, the question and its response provide no 'quick fix' for the complexities made apparent. The question surely leads in a direction unimagined by popular advocates of the application of business principles to education.

In addition to the particular meanings already addressed, conventional understandings of 'control' in curriculum discourse are turned inside out by this response to the question of customer. 'Control' continues to exist, to be sure, but its locus is partitioned between customers (pupils) and others (for example, teachers, administrators, parents). This reasonable response to the insistent market question concerning customer identity alters profoundly the manner in which schooling and curriculum are considered in society. After this question, nothing can be the same.

This essay into some imagined meanings for curriculum embedded in the market metaphor is modest, tentative, and exploratory. Like other metaphors, this one surely will collapse if pushed far enough. But how far is that 'push too far'? I believe the limits lie beyond the present horizon of thought. Whatever distance matters less than another significant realisation.

Essential market questions need not diminish nor demean curriculum inquiry. Indeed, insistence on responses just to one question, 'Who is the curriculum customer?' can rejuvenate thought and revive a leaden discourse - between us curriculum professionals, as well as in conversations and debates with and among politicians, parents, officials in business and work, citizens, and ourselves.

Propositions and suggestions proffered here cry out for elaboration. This rethinking will not distort principled portrayals of schools in a democratic society. Analyses rigorously using market terms, rather than language specific to manufacturing, will likely yield prominent benefits to curriculum and schooling. We must be prudent. We will need to avoid confusions such as ones between 'curriculum customers' and 'consumers'. In our use of the language of the market, we also should be able to rejoin our professional efforts with those of the general public fundamentally to reform education. I invite you to join me in the pursuit of these possibilities.

Chapter 10

The triangular relationship of the teacher, knowledge, and the child: accountability in action

Elinor A. Scheirer

Children's acquisition of knowledge has always been a central focus of the primary school from its inception by modern societies as an instrument for the socialisation of the young. Its goals have traditionally included the development of literacy and numeracy and exposure to facts and concepts deemed necessary by society for successful adult functioning, regardless of the pedagogical techniques and curricular organisations which may have been in vogue at a particular time.

Against this background the calls of recent years for instruction in 'the basics' or for a core curriculum raise several issues. Without arguing the implications in these statements that certain primary school programs must not address 'the basics', this paper examines how teachers might reassure political decision-makers and the public at large that knowledge acquisition is indeed occurring in classrooms. It asserts that there are ways in which children and teachers confront knowledge and that there are qualitative differences among these ways which affect learning. The acquisition of skills and knowledge, then, is not simply a matter of 'calling for' the return to some bygone day when teachers 'taught' what all agreed was necessary and children learned it.

Teachers and researchers concerned about classroom interactions must, rather, engage in rigorous analysis of the processes that accompany such learning. They must question in what ways preset knowledge requirements for all children can be met when individuals vary and educational settings substantially differ. They must seek a balance among three factors in the learning process: the nature of knowledge in the many discipline areas, the demands of teaching, and the needs of children.

The dilemmas associated with knowledge acquisition in school settings also must recognise that any complete analysis also rests on describing the sociological and political aspects involved with the definitions of knowledge and its construction (see, for example, Anyon, 1981; Apple and King, 1979). However, while this chapter acknowledges the crucial contribution a developed sociology of knowledge can make to an enlightened view of how to empower children cognitively, it limits discussion here to the way in which teachers in classrooms might consider their tasks more immediately. The chapter focuses on how teachers might approach the knowledges and skills which are the common media of exchange in classrooms regardless of social class, even though its recommendations surely can also impact the development of a sociological sensitivity to knowledge construction writ large.

The major premise is that the teacher participates in a triangular relationship with the child and with knowledge in the learning situation:

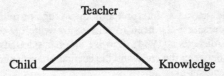

In giving life to this relationship, the teacher acts as a bridge between the children and knowledge; the teacher both interprets knowledge for the child in order to facilitate learning and helps the child make personal meaning of the knowledge confronted.

Indeed, the teacher also needs to develop a deep and intricate dialogue with the various forms of knowledge as a prerequisite to facilitating children's learning. The teacher must have interacted with knowledge. To paraphrase Piaget, one builds increasingly more complex and more powerful cognitive structures in order to understand the world. Knowledge, therefore, is not merely a passive phenomenon but is something to be interpreted to oneself and thence to children in the process of creating psychological meaning.

Achieving such a dialogue with knowledge is not an easy process and is a crucial task for both pre-service and in-service teacher education. However, because the central concern here is how the teacher helps the *child* interact with knowledge, this discussion assumes that the teacher is already somewhat comfortable with the dimensions of knowledge with which the child must be engaged.

THE TEACHER AS INTERPRETER OF KNOWLEDGE

Ayers (1986) offers a rich metaphor which helps to explain the role of the teacher in helping children confront knowledge - that of the midwife. He notes that personal interaction, communication, is 'the heart and soul of a relationship that can unlock potential and power' (p. 49).

This view is akin to Martin Buber's (1958) notion of the development of an 'I-thou', mutual relationship; the learner engages intimately with the material at hand in order to make sense of it and thus to be empowered by understanding its meaning. Knowledge acquisition is active and involves children in construction and reconstruction, with the teacher as an 'interactor' (Ayers, 1986, p. 50) who activates others in their engagement with 'object matter'.

Ayers (1986) describes the good teacher who asserts the need for balance between content and the curriculum on the one hand and children and their needs, concerns, and experiences on the other. Such teachers recognise that:

> 'it is their own vital relationship with children that is at the heart of the educational enterprise ... They are able to communicate to their students in a thousand ways, "you are of central importance here", "your work is honoured here", "your discoveries and growth are respected here", and, finally, "you are the very reason we are here"' (p. 50).

The role of the teacher as interpreter of knowledge or midwife, to children as they learn underscores the need for discussion which avoids the use of false dichotomies. Alexander (1984) likewise emphasises that dichotomies which force choices between the child and the curriculum risk simplistic and shallow educational decision-making.

Indeed, Dewey's (1956) *The Child and the Curriculum* argues this same point:

> 'When this happens a really serious practical problem - that of interaction - is transformed into an unreal, and hence insoluble, theoretic problem. Instead of seeing the educative steadily and as a whole, we see conflicting terms. We get the case of the child *vs.* the curriculum; of the individual nature *vs.* social culture. Below all other divisions in pedagogic opinion lies this opposition' (pp. 4-5).

Dewey asks us to:

> 'abandon the notion of subject-matter as something fixed and ready-made in itself, outside the child's experience; cease thinking of the child's experience as also something hard and fast; see it as something fluent, embryonic, vital; and we realise that the child and the curriculum are simply two limits which define a single process' (p. 11).

The child and subject matter reflect a dialectic interaction, presumably with the conjunction 'and' deliberately selected.

Portraying the teacher as an interpreter of knowledge with children is strongly reminiscent of Hawkins' (1973) ideas regarding the 'triangular relationship of teacher, student, and materials' (p. 364), so eloquently shared in a Leicestershire workshop twenty years ago. Hawkins proposes materials and the experience of them by teachers and children as a means by which they may communicate with each other about the process of learning; thus, the child 'comes alive for the teacher as well as the teacher for the child' (pp. 369-370). The teacher and the child are 'in *it* together' (p. 373). From such interaction, the teacher is then able to gather the information upon which to provide the selective feedback that furthers learning and to diagnose what children need as a guide for future instructional decisions.

This relationship takes on added meaning in the context of a time which stresses knowledge and skills perceived as fixed entities to be acquired by the child, with the teacher often merely acting as engineer. Materials have so often become inert sheets of paper which represent manufactured abstractions rather than relate to real experiences. In such a situation there is little for the teacher and child to discuss meaningfully, as the diagram below indicates:

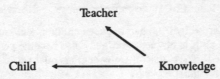

The most many teachers can hope to do in this case is to help in passing along the knowledge in its disseminated forms with the addition of explanatory footnotes. They explain to children what they have been told must be taught in much the same way as it has been distributed to them. The diagram then becomes:

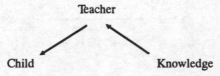

Because little meaningful discussion occurs and hence little learning beyond recognition and recall, the triangular relationship must shift. The teacher needs to function as an active intermediary between the materials or knowledge and the child to become an interpreter of knowledge for the child:

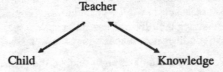

This process requires presentation of the preset knowledge and skills that may be required by government agencies in ways which promote children's learning. And, since interaction and dialogue are central to active involvement with knowledge, the process then becomes:

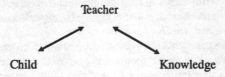

As the child becomes more of an investigator or teacher on his or her own and becomes involved with ideas, the relationship evolves to:

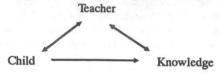

Thus the teacher bridges the gap between children and knowledge so that the knowledge which is to be 'acquired' may also become personally meaningful and thus 'learned'. The teacher thereby demonstrates accountability as an active and highly professional process.

For both teacher and child, the engagement with knowledge and with each other would ultimately be shown as:

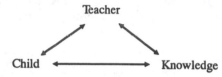

Dynamic and ongoing interaction would be fundamental so that meaning and empowerment would grow.

THE TEACHER AND CHILD WORKING TOGETHER

Several views of this interpretive function of teaching may lend clarity to the discussion, though they are hardly more than suggestive of what this process might mean. This section supports the assertion that there are deliberate, careful, powerful ways for teachers to work with children in promoting their intellectual growth while engaging their lives, ideas, and experiences.

Dewey (1956) outlines how teachers may view classroom interactions:

'Just as two points define a straight line, so the present standpoint of the child and the facts and truths of studies define instruction. It is continuous reconstruction, moving from the child's present experience out into that represented by the organised bodies of truth that we call studies' (p. 11).

Subject matter and the child's present experience compromise one reality and so cannot war with each other. 'Development does not mean just getting something out of the mind. It is a development of experience and into experience that is really wanted' (p. 18).

Hawkins (James, 1983) suggests how such a perspective might operate within the area of science. Fieldwork and investigations provide primary children with active experiences so that they might become *involved in* the subject matter. Teachers reflect a trust in the subject matter and a commitment to it which are based on their own attempts at understanding its concepts. They often talk with children only informally in the course of instruction as they develop 'case histories of what [is being] learned' (p. 365). Such a process is not only appropriate in science but can also lead to other content areas. 'Every subject leads to others. The great art is to know some of those interconnecting pathways ... in order to entice children to go along and discover more' (p. 365). The teacher's own relationship with knowledge therefore continuously grows far beyond the analysis which guided the initial instructional efforts. Hawkins' teacher has developed a close and dynamic relationship with knowledge in which children also participate; teacher and children, then, work together to extend the boundaries of their own understandings.

Barnes (1976) examines carefully the knowledge component of the triangular relationship in order to characterise the various roles teachers might assume with children. He describes how a teacher's view of knowledge leads to particular communication patterns with children which in turn encourage certain kinds of learning. The transmission teachers and interpretation teachers markedly differ from each other in their interactions with learners.

Interpretation teachers believe that knowledge exists 'in the knower's ability to organise thought and action', and they perceive their task to be 'the setting up of a dialogue in which the learner can reshape his knowledge through interaction with others' (Barnes, 1976, p. 144). The dialogue, through either talking or writing, enables the development of everyday action knowledge as opposed to esoteric school knowledge. This collaborative approach uses speech and writing so that children might explore ideas, relate their new knowledge to their own purposes and interests, and thereby become independent learners. Barnes' teacher who interprets knowledge *with* children actively sets up dialogue, negotiation, and collaboration. Class participants use language as a medium through which they expand knowledge boundaries and reflect upon knowledge so as to control it and be empowered by it.

Rowland (1984) shares this interest in the child's point of view regarding how knowledge is confronted in school. The methodology of his investigation into the nature of children's thinking and into their attempts to control their own learning also depicts a process which teachers might use in responding to children. While principally a research procedure, his discussions and conversations with children about their work and their understandings and his reflecting upon children's understanding suggest teaching practice which can bring about children's interpretation of knowledge. The themes of Hawkins and Barnes surface again in Rowland's discussions; the teacher uses dialogue both to diagnose what children may need to further their learning and to shape and reshape understanding *with* them. Indeed, central to their conversation and collaboration is how both teacher and children respect each other's interpretations or constructions of subject matter.

Similarly, Armstrong's (1980) account of a primary classroom indicates how reflective observation might facilitate the teacher's role as interpreter of knowledge. His type of analysis of children's learning, while also borne of research, clearly leads to a perspective on teaching. This is teaching which recognises children's efforts in making meaning of experience through engaging them with rich materials and actively using their thoughts as starting points for further learning. Close observation provides the data about the children's experience which subsequently shape the teacher's role.

THE INTERPRETIVE ROLE AND ACCOUNTABILITY

The title of this chapter promised to connect concerns for accountability with the role of the teacher as interpreter of knowledge. In detailing the triangular relationship of the teacher, knowledge and the child, there is also implicit the assertion that knowledge is indeed important in school activity. However, the triangular relationship also asserts that knowledge is not pre-eminent but is only one of the entities with which the other two must interact if learning is to occur.

Presumably, accountability refers to the need for teachers to accomplish that which society charges them to accomplish. The nature of the statements of goals and objectives thus becomes important, for if they represent general skills, abilities, and understandings, they are not inconsistent with the teaching process this paper has sketched. Both American and English statements indicate such general goals and objectives, though there may be requirements that children demonstrate their attainment in particular ways. Therefore, it is argued that teachers can be accountable while also working with children to help them interact with knowledge meaningfully.

Such a teaching role is not easy to assume. It requires that teachers first examine their own learning experiences, their own relationships with knowledge. They then must approach their interactions with children so as to engage children with knowledge. They must accept the variability among children since any genuine encounters with knowledge must begin with the children. The 'interpretive' nature of the role comes alive as teachers interpret the learning process with children, share and discuss experiences with children, and enable children to make sense of their own confrontations with knowledge. The role is therefore highly demanding because it requires of teachers constant analysis and decision-making.

What this paper has described is therefore not an anti-intellectual process for teachers to follow in their work with children. It is very much knowledge-based, but with the requirement that both the teacher and child interact with knowledge and with each other in relation to knowledge. The description is not at all new to educational thinking, for as early as Dewey (1956) the process was laid out clearly. The argument goes beyond a discussion of teaching in the abstract to a concern with teaching subject matter with 'a sense of style', as Hawkins has expressed it (James, 1983, p. 362).

Thus, we are not faced with a simplistic problem of either focusing on children and their learning or on attainments in the content areas. These concerns cannot be polarised but must be considered in their relation to each other and as the teacher serves to bring about that interaction. Furthermore, we must remember that 'the more we hear from the educational researcher, the learning theorist, and the developmental psychologist, the more we stand in awe of the learner' (Ayers, 1986, p. 51).

Under the pressures of bureaucratic statements regarding curriculum objectives and, implicitly, curriculum content, many of us seem to need the reminder of what is indeed necessary in teaching and what remains problematic. The rationale for our work is there. And we need not be in conflict with those who worry with us about children's learning.

References

Alexander, R. J. (1984) *Primary teaching*, Holt, Rinehart and Winston, London.

Anyon, J. (1981) Social class and school knowledge, *Curriculum Inquiry*, (11) 1, pp. 3-42.

Apple, M. W. and King, N. (1979) Economics and control in everyday school life, in M. W. Apple, (ed.) *Ideology and Curriculum*, Routledge and Kegan Paul, London.

Armstrong, M. (1980) *Closely Observed Children: The Diary of a Primary Classroom*, Writers and Readers, London.

Ayers, W. (1986) About teaching and teachers: thinking about teachers and the curriculum, *Harvard Educational Review*, (56) 1, pp. 49-51.

Barnes, D. (1976) *From Communication to Curriculum*, Penguin, Harmondsworth, England.

Buber, M. (1958) *I and Thou* (2nd edition), Scribner's, New York.

Dewey, J. (1956) *The Child and the Curriculum* and *The School and Society*, University of Chicago, Chicago.

Hawkins, D. (1973) The triangular relationship of teacher, student, and materials, in C. E. Silberman (ed.), *The Open Classroom Reader*, Random House, New York.

James, T. (1983) Teacher of teachers, companion of children: an interview with David Hawkins, *Phi Delta Kappan*, (64), pp. 362-365.

Rowland, S. (1984) *The Enquiring Classroom: An Approach to Understanding Children's Learning*, Falmer, Lewes, England.

Chapter 11

Assessing, recording and reporting achievement - after the Education Reform Act

Stephen Munby

INTRODUCTION

The current situation concerning the assessment, recording and reporting of achievement remains one of uncertainty and of shifting ground. At the time of writing, the development of *standard assessment tasks* (SATs) for key stage one are about to be trialled whilst SATs for key stage three are in a very early stage of development. The regulations for National Curriculum Assessment Arrangements are not yet available and the regulations for reporting individual achievement are only available in draft form. Standardisation training has yet to begin in earnest and there are clear moves from the Secretary of State for Education to look for ways of diminishing the workload of teachers attempting to implement the considerable demands of the Education Reform Act.

Because of this changing situation, any attempt to write about the relationship between records of achievement and the assessment of the National Curriculum constitutes a rather foolhardy venture and may prove to be out of date even before it is published. Nevertheless, since teachers have been attempting to implement *teacher assessments* (TAs) since September 1989 in mathematics, science and English with Year 1 children and in mathematics and science with Year 7 students, it is imperative that we analyse the situation as it currently stands rather than waiting for two or three years when we might have a more complete picture. This chapter is a personal analysis of the emerging themes and is written to facilitate thinking concerning possible strategies for holding on to the positive benefits of records of achievement while implementing the assessment, recording and reporting requirements of the National Curriculum.

VALUES AND RATIONALE

When it comes to evaluating any educational initiative, one of the crucial questions to ask is whether it is likely to improve the educational experience of young people. It is my belief that by far the most powerful argument in favour of records of achievement is that they can enhance the learning and development of students and that the main rationale for records of achievement is that, in their 'formative process', they attempt to address the following six basic learning needs.

1. I need to know what I am doing well, what I need to improve and what progress I am making

If the only feedback on a piece of work that I receive from my teacher is in the form of a mark or a grade it is unlikely to help my learning. What is a grade 'C' actually telling learners? All it is really saying to them is that in the mind of their teacher they have done worse than those who received A or B, and better than those who received D or E. It does not tell them in what way they have done better or worse, nor what their strengths and weaknesses actually are; it does not tell them how to improve nor on what aspect of their work they need to concentrate in the future. In contrast, the processes involved in records of achievement are designed to make assessment more diagnostic and to provide detailed and meaningful feedback to learners so that they are aware of their own individual progress and of what they need to do to improve further.

2. I need to have my achievements recognised

It can be relatively difficult for those of us who were, and are, successful academically to understand what it is like to be regarded as a low achiever. However, on a recent skiing holiday I experienced what it was like to be a 'low achiever'. By the third day of ski school I had moved from being one of the better skiers in the group to one of the worst. My first reaction to this situation was to try harder, and when I realised that in spite of my efforts I was still one of the worst in the group I began to feel demoralised and to say to myself: 'Who cares about skiing anyway!' What I needed as a learner was to have my achievements pointed out and for the ski instructor to help me to set some personal targets that I could achieve. Although my attainment was small compared to most of the others in the group, I was still making progress and I needed to have my achievements positively recognised in order to be a motivated learner. I needed, in fact, to have a ski instructor who believed in the processes of records of achievement.

3. I need to know what is expected of me

It is, I believe, a basic learning need to know what is expected of you as a learner. When I was a student at school I was often assessed without knowing beforehand what the teacher was looking for. To be assessed without knowing the criteria upon which you are being assessed is unlikely to help you to learn. If there are specific objectives or attainment targets that apply to a particular course, then those attainment targets need to be communicated to the students.

4. I need to have some short-term achievable targets

If students have to wait a long time for feedback, their learning can often lose its way and they can soon become unmotivated. When I was a student at school the assessments were usually at the end of courses when it was too late to do anything about it. Part of the rationale for records of achievement is that targets should be set which are understandable to the learner and which are achievable in a fairly short space of time, thus providing regular incentives and ongoing feedback.

5. I need to feel valued, involved and respected

Part of the rationale of records of achievement is the belief that students will learn more effectively if they feel valued and are actively involved in the learning and assessment process. The records of achievement process is based upon the principle that students are individuals with their own individual learning needs and that each student matters so much that they should be given the opportunity to express their own views about their achievements and progress.

6. I need to evaluate my own learning and to develop strategies to improve it

A key part of the records of achievement process is that students should be given the opportunity to review their own learning and to set future targets. The ability to evaluate what we have learned is an important skill which we often need as adults and we do not usually have a 'teacher' around to do it for us. If all of the assessment and all the reporting is done *for* students by the teacher, when will the students have the opportunity to develop that ability for themselves? Frankly, issuing records of achievement to school-leavers is largely a waste of time unless the students know how to use them, and that is why it is so important that they be actively involved in ongoing self-evaluation and in recording their own achievement.

Moreover, the reviewing process itself is an aid to effective learning. The reviewing process, by definition, involves self-assessment and engages the learner in thinking about what they have learned. At its best the reviewing process can reinforce learning by helping students to make sense of their experiences and to gain a better understanding not only of the work that has been covered but also of their own strengths and weaknesses.

EMERGING ISSUES

Assessing the national curriculum

The arrangements for assessing the national curriculum which were proposed in the report of the Task Group on Assessment and Testing (TGAT) (DES/Welsh Office, 1987) have been largely accepted by the Department of Education and Science. The assessment arrangements involve both teacher assessments (devised by teachers, continuous and internal to the school) and standard assessment tasks (devised by development agencies). The national curriculum assessment system is, therefore, not essentially about testing at the age of seven, eleven, fourteen and sixteen; it is, rather, about assessment from five to sixteen which is moderated and standardised by SATs at the end of each key stage.

At the time of writing, we know that all students near the end of each key stage should, unless they are exempted, experience SATs but, as yet, we do not know what a SAT actually is. The specifications for SATs, however, suggest that they should:

- be administered by teachers as a natural part of their normal mode of teaching;
- be easily administered, scored and recorded by teachers;
- include written testing and a variety of other assessment measures including oral, practical and graphic work done individually and in groups;
- produce standardised results across all schools and all age groups.(see SEAC, 1988 and 1989a).

Three fundamental questions arise from a consideration of these specifications:

Will SATs work?

If there should be no marked distinction between what students experience during ordinary lesson time and what they experience during a SAT this means that they should be learning through a SAT in the same way that they learn through ordinary classroom work. One of the problems that may arise from this is how much aid a teacher should give to students. Under normal circumstances, if a student were struggling during an activity the teacher would probably intervene to help. How much intervention, however, will be permitted from teachers during SATs?

It has been suggested by some that the teacher should still intervene during a SAT in order to ensure that the student completes the activity successfully, but that the amount of help provided by the teacher would determine whether or not the student had attained the appropriate level. Such a scenario would create considerable problems for standardisation and moderation. If, however, no help is to be provided by the teacher then there will clearly be a marked difference for the students between their normal classroom work and SATs and they may find themselves spending three or four weeks during the summer term at the end of each key stage carrying out activities in which they receive no support from their teachers.

If SATs are to involve a wide variety of assessment techniques, including oral work, then the problem of finding the time to carry out the oral assessments in fair conditions becomes considerable. Moreover, there are undoubted classroom management problems if teachers are going to assess group work and individual attainment in large classes of students. These difficulties can, I believe, be largely overcome through careful planning and through developments in teaching and learning styles but not without time for planning meetings and the provision of high quality in-service training, both of which have considerable resource implications.

In addition, the problems of attempting to standardise SATs so that a level 2 in a mathematics attainment target attained by a seven year-old student in an inner-city multi-ethnic primary school in a cross-curricular SAT is exactly the same as a level 2 in the same mathematical attainment target attained by a fourteen year-old in a subject-specific SAT in a shire comprehensive school are so complex that it is no surprise that the SEAC and the DES have not yet suggested how it is going to be done.

The fact is that the concept of SATs is a very laudable one, since written testing tends to overemphasise the importance of cognitive ability and memory recall while discriminating against those who have writing difficulties and those who tend to perform less well under pressure. Nevertheless, the problems of ensuring objectivity and lack of gender or race bias combined with the immense practical difficulties of implementing SATs makes their future by no means certain. Written tests are cheaper, more accurate, easier to compare and less complex to moderate. No doubt when the National Curriculum was first announced many traditionalists were anticipating the return of brown envelopes with written tests inside them and were disappointed when the proposals of the TGAT report were accepted. However, if standard assessment tasks prove too difficult to implement, they may yet get their wish.

How will the relationship between SATs and teacher assessments develop?

As SEAC have already made clear (SEAC, 1989), whenever a teacher assessment comes up against a SAT result the SAT result is preferred. However, to counteract the reaction from many that this marginalises the teacher assessment and constitutes an attack on both the formative process and the professionalism of teachers, SEAC are emphasising three points:

 i. that the SATs will be implemented and assessed by teachers and are still, therefore, in a very real way teacher assessments;

ii. that the SATs will probably only sample the attainment targets and whenever a SAT has not been used to assess an attainment then the teacher assessment is the result that will be recorded;

iii. that the teacher can appeal if a particular child has performed much better during the year than during the SATs.

All of these points go some way to diminishing fears that the assessment will be concentrated on three or four weeks of activities at the end of each key stage, but two important concerns remain. First of all, if the SATs are only going to sample attainment targets and yet be preferred to teacher assessments whenever they do, then many teachers will surely attempt to teach to the tests. It is all too easy to envisage teachers pouring over past SATs and attempting to predict what will be covered in next year's papers so that they can ensure high scores for their children, thus reinforcing the notion that it is how you perform in the SATs that counts.

Secondly, in spite of all SEAC's claims to the contrary, their proposals will still marginalise teacher assessments unless SATs are seen to be primarily an initial checking mechanism for teachers to help to standardise their assessments across the country. If this is the case, then the importance of SATs should diminish rather than increase as teachers become more confident and we should see a gradual 'withering away' of SATs to be replaced by LEA standardisation training combined with local and regional monitoring and moderation procedures (shades of CSE?)

Will each Statement of Attainment (SoA) need to be assessed?

At the time of writing there still seems to be a determination that all SoAs should be assessed as discrete entities and the current SAT activities seem to reinforce this notion. This side, however, is generating a 'checklist mentality' amongst teachers who are ticking each SoA off as 'experienced' and/or 'attained'. If, however, SoAs do not have to be assessed discretely but are only there to help teachers to have an idea as to what constitutes attainment of a target at a particular level then the assessment and the recording process can become more flexible. This is crucial if the assessment is going to be genuinely learner-centred and learning-centred.

Recording and reporting achievement

There has been much discussion in the educational press concerning the future of records of achievement and there have been suggestions that they are either 'dead' or 'terminally ill', as a result of changes in government thinking. As is now becoming clear, the DES are not going to require schools to report on anything other than National Curriculum attainment, though they are actively encouraging schools to record achievement in its broader sense (DES/Welsh Office, 1990).

As is now well known, the Report of the Records of Achievement National Steering Committee (DES/Welsh Office, 1989) which proposed national guidelines for records of achievement in secondary schools, has been rejected by the DES, in spite of the fact that the RANSC Report was very well received and in spite of SEAC's firm conclusion, after widespread consultation, that there was 'strong and widespread support for the nationwide use of records of achievement in schools, underpinned by regulations' (SEAC, 1989b).

The determination by the DES to reject their earlier policy statement (DES/Welsh Office, 1984) and to refuse to implement national arrangements for records of achievement is not only flying in the face of the overwhelmingly positive response to the initiative from educationalists and employers, but also means that some students will not receive what I believe is their entitlement, namely:

- opportunities and encouragement to assess themselves, to review their own learning and to set their own learning targets; and

- involvement in developing with their teachers an on-going record of their achievements, within and outside school, and to receive a summary record of their achievements when they leave.

Nevertheless, in spite of the duplicity of the DES on this matter, where records of achievement have already taken root, they will continue to flourish in both their process and product, due to the considerable benefits schools have experienced in terms of increased student and teacher motivation, more appropriate curriculum planning and delivery, and better teacher-student relationships.

Some schools, however, are currently attempting to keep their records of achievement totally divorced from the National Curriculum, in order to ensure that records of achievement remain pure and untainted by nationally prescribed levels of attainment. Levels of attainment will, they argue, demotivate students by reinforcing feelings of failure amongst many and will lead to a narrow, sterile assessment system. They therefore see records of achievement as needing to steer clear of National Curriculum assessment arrangements and operating exclusively in the areas of cross-curricular and personal achievements. As I have argued elsewhere (Munby, 1989 and Munby, 1990), this approach, though seemingly laudable, is extremely unwise and unhelpful. It is, by default, marginalising records of achievement and depriving them of their key role in providing coherence to all assessment and recording, both within and beyond the National Curriculum.

The fact is that the draft regulations on reporting individual pupil achievement (DES/Welsh Office, 1990) are minimal requirements and most parents and students will want to know far more than a set of National Curriculum scores. The only way forward which is genuinely helpful for all concerned is a whole-school approach to assessing, recording and reporting achievement. The distinction between attainment and achievement is crucial here: attainment + context = achievement, and the context includes how I feel about what I have done and what I did this time compared to what I did last time. Moreover, achievement is much broader than attainment and includes personal and out-of-school achievement.

The assessment of cross-curricular skills

Is there a potential conflict between the Report of the Records of Achievement National Steering Committee (RANSC) which emphasises the importance of assessing and/or recording general skills and personal achievement and the national curriculum statutory orders which are couched in subject-specific terms?

I have written elsewhere in much more detail on this issue (Munby *et al.*, 1989) but a few observations can be made at this point:

1. The national curriculum is not the whole curriculum. The National Curriculum Council in its Interim Report on Cross-Curricular Issues (see NCC, 1989) recommends that cross-curricular skills, such as oracy and study skills, should be promoted throughout all or most of the curriculum and that schools should map their curriculum to decide how best to develop cross-curricular skills.

2. We should not be trying to assess everything in terms of attainment targets and levels. The concept of a level 6 in sensitivity or a level 8 in reliability is appalling.

3. The assessment of cross-curricular or general skills can only make sense within a context. The statement 'can solve problems' is banal and meaningless unless it is linked to a context. If general skills such as study skills are important in science and are developed in science then they should be assessed in the context of science not divorced to personal and social education lessons only.

4. There need be no ultimate conflict between the demands of records of achievement and the requirements of the National Curriculum as far as the assessment of cross-curricular skills is concerned. As I have argued elsewhere:

   Whenever an assessable skill is demonstrated within a context it may be assessed and recorded. If that skill happens to be linked to a national curriculum attainment target for a particular subject and it is demonstrated within that subject context then it can be part of national curriculum assessment and be reported on accordingly. If it is not linked to any national curriculum attainment target, then the skill can still be recognised and, if appropriate, reported either through an interim summary or final summary record of achievement. Schools will need to carry out a careful curriculum audit to ensure that such general skills are covered in a coherent way and are assessed appropriately (Munby, 1989, pp. 199-200)

Monitoring and inspection

It now seems likely that there will be no separate accreditation requirements for records of achievement. Ultimately, therefore, unless local education authorities (LEAs) develop an assessment, recording and reporting policy which builds in the formative processes of records of achievement and unless governing bodies accept that policy there will be no compulsion for schools even to attempt to implement many of the learning principles outlined at the beginning of this chapter. If, however, a local education authority policy based upon the principles of records of achievement is accepted, then LEA inspectors will be monitoring schools to ensure that processes such as self-assessment and teacher-student dialogue are being implemented. If this is the case, we may have a scenario which involves records of achievement for students and for teachers and for schools.

Students have non-negotiable parameters acting upon them (for example, the national curriculum statutory orders), but within those they may find they have some flexibility to negotiate their own individual learning programmes. They enter into dialogue with their teachers who are both assessors and supportive reviewers and the students receive a record of achievement, with appropriate future targets. Likewise, the teachers have non-negotiable parameters acting upon them but within those they have flexibility to develop their own individual teaching style and to further their own professional development. The teachers enter into dialogue with their appraisers who are both assessors and supportive reviewers and they receive a record of achievement, with agreed future targets. School governing bodies and senior management teams have some flexibility within the non-negotiable parameters. They enter into dialogue with LEA inspectors who are both assessors and supportive reviewers and the school receives a record of achievement and negotiates future objectives.

This model of records of achievement for all will stand or fall on the quality of the dialogue between the various parties. Just as the students need to develop self-assessment skills, so do the teachers. Likewise, the school, and the departments within it, will also need to develop self-monitoring skills. If the teacher is an assessor but not a supportive reviewer the students may soon lose interest and feel undervalued; if the appraisers do not have reviewing skills we may have even more teachers opting out and leaving the profession and if the inspectors are not supportive reviewers we may see schools opting out from local education authorities altogether.

There is, indeed, much uncertainty about the future but there remain some grounds of optimism and it is possible, I believe, to implement the assessment, recording and reporting of achievement after the Education Reform Act while holding on firmly to the learning principles outlined at the beginning of this chapter.

WAYS FORWARD

1. Local education authorities need to develop assessment, recording and reporting policies which are based upon the principles of records of achievement and which give guidance to schools as to how they might develop their whole-school assessment policies.

2. Schools need to develop whole-school assessment, recording and reporting policies. These policies should include such aspects as:

(a) the school's rationale and principles for assessment;

(b) general guidelines and framework for department/class teacher assessment policies;

(c) general guidelines for pastoral teams and for the production of statements of personal achievement by students and tutors;

(d) guidelines on how achievement and attainment is to be summarised and a framework/format for reports (in line with government requirements);

(e) strategies for involving parents and governors in the assessment, recording and reporting process, as appropriate;

(f) the general skills and personal achievement which the school wishes to develop and record (linked to a curriculum audit);

(g) the assessment of responsibilities of:

(i) assessment co-ordinator/s

(ii) heads of department

(iii) classroom teachers

(iv) tutors;

(h) guidelines and strategies for monitoring and evaluating assessment, recording and reporting at all levels.

3. Support work and in-service training (INSET) in subject areas and in curriculum development should be integrated with support and INSET in assessment. This has implications for how advisers and advisory teachers carry out their work. It is no longer appropriate to deliver, for example, INSET in English without also covering the assessment implications.

4. We should not be waiting for SATs to finally appear on the scene before we address assessment issues. Teachers should be supported as soon as possible

in ways of integrating ongoing assessment and recording into their teaching, whatever age group or subject they teach and they need to become accustomed to producing reports based upon clear criteria. The more teachers develop these skills and techniques the more they will be able to cope with the requirements of the National Curriculum. The way forward for teachers in the next few years, irrespective of what form the SATs eventually take, is to develop ongoing teacher assessment and recording mechanisms which: are integral to learning; involve the student in self-assessment and achievable target-setting; are linked to National Curriculum attainment targets and programmes of study, where available; recognise and celebrate a wide range of achievements, including cross-curricular skills and personal achievement; and are part of a whole-school and department assessment, recording and reporting policy.

5. We should be prepared to compromise on terminology but not on rationale. 'Profiling' is no longer an appropriate word to use and even terms like 'records of achievement' and 'reviewing' seem to be giving way to terms such as 'assessing, recording and reporting' and 'action-planning'. Personally, I am relatively happy to change my terminology as long as I can hold on to the essential principles and processes which used to be part of good practice in profiling and record of achievement.

Some people see the Education Reform Act as a threat to records of achievement. In one sense they are correct and there may well be many schools who fail to address the formative process of records of achievement and who produce nothing more than glorified reports containing mainly numbers and levels. However, there is nothing in the Education Reform Act to prevent local education authorities, schools and teachers from implementing the six learning principles, outlined at the beginning of this chapter, within and beyond the national curriculum.

The Pilot Records of Achievement in Schools Evaluation (PRAISE) report which evaluated the nine DES-funded pilot schemes for records of achievement stated that their evidence confirmed: ' ... a continuing consensus that records of achievement can raise the standard of pupils' learning by raising their involvement in, their commitment to, and their enjoyment of, the educational process' (PRAISE Team, 1988).

If we believe that statement we will make sure that the processes of records of achievement will underpin how we operate at classroom, school and LEA level and in doing so the people with whom we work will not only feel more valued they are also more likely to be effective learners.

References

DES/Welsh Office, (1987) *The Report of the Task Group on Assessment and Testing*.

DES/Welsh Office, (1989) *Records of Achievement - A Final Report*.

DES/Welsh Office, (1990) *The Education (Individual Pupil's Achievements) (Information) Regulations 1990*. January 5th.

Munby, S. *et al. (1989) Assessing and Recording Achievement*, Blackwell, Oxford.

Munby, S. (1990) Profiling and Records of Achievement in the 1990s, in *Training and Development Bulletin*, national Institute for Careers Education and Counselling, 37.

NCC, (1989) *Newsletter of the National Curriculum Council*, June.

PRAISE Team (1988) *Records of Achievement. Report of the National Evaluation of Pilot Schemes*, HMSO, London.

SEAC (1988) *Development of Standard Assessment Tasks for pupils are the End of the First Key Stage of the National Curriculum, Secondary Examinations and Assessment Council*.

SEAC (1989a) *Development of Standard Assessment Tasks for pupils at the End of the Third Key Stage of the National Curriculum, Secondary Examinations and Assessment Council*.

SEAC (1989b) *Records of Achievement*. Letter from Philip Halsey to the Secretaries of State concerning SEAC's recommendations for records of achievement.

SEAC (1989c) *National Curriculum: Assessment Arrangements*. SEAC's advice to the Secretary of State, dated 12 December 1989.

Chapter 12

Product or process: what is effective learning?

Marcella L Kysilka

Historically, American educators have debated the issue of product or process as the foundation of curriculum organisation of American public school curriculum. These debates were fuelled by a changing society and the search for appropriate education for an ever increasing and diversified body of students. For example, in the early 1900s, the public concern was over the ultra conservative approach of the schools and the fact that the schools were not keeping pace with the changing times. Concerns were raised over the excessive amount of rigour and formal, narrow-minded approaches to very traditional content areas. Questions were raised as to how well the American schools were meeting the needs of a variety of students, not just academically able and professionally oriented ones. The call was for more domestic sciences, and programmes in the manual arts. During the 1930s questions were raised again about the adherence to a traditional curriculum focused on sets of skills and a given body of knowledge. Behavioural researchers were encouraging educators to experiment with organisation of curriculum including ideas such as core curriculum, broad-fields curriculum, and experienced-centred curriculum. All of these approaches were designed to help the students see relationships between what they were learning and experiencing, alternatives to memorisation and recall which predominated much of what was happening in the schools. (Parker and Rubin, 1966)

When the Soviet Union successfully launched Sputnik, the American people once again expressed their dismay over the inadequacies of the public school curriculum. Educators were encouraged to restructure and reorganise the curriculum. The 'product-process' debate became heated. Scientists, mathematicians, psychologists and educators argued about how to best teach science and mathematics to K-12 students. Curriculum programmes after curriculum programmes were designed to include specific scientific and mathematical processes as integral parts of the 'new' science and mathematics curricula. These programmes were funded by the federal government on the assumption that they would help students to think and process information in science and mathematics more effectively and efficiently. The government also funded training programmes for teachers, to help them learn how to use the new programmes in their classrooms. However, despite the efforts of the science community, the educators, and the government, the 'new' science and mathematics curricula were not successful, that is, American children were not better scientists and mathematicians. There were several reasons for the failure of these programmes to achieve the lofty goals set by the developers and hoped for by the government:

1. Programmes were implemented faster than teachers were adequately trained to teach them. Consequently, many teachers compromised the goals of the programmes and continued to teach what they knew how to teach and what they understood.

2. Much of the material was designed for the more able youngster. There was not sufficient diversity in levels of difficulty to accommodate the majority of students enrolled in the public schools. They became frustrated and their parents became critical about the curriculum.

3. There was a rising tide of concern over civil rights issues, including appropriate education opportunities for all students. Also, America 'caught up' in the space race and her social problems at home were escalating. The government started funding social programmes and sharply decreased the amount of dollars spent on science and mathematics education. Funds were used to establish and enhance programmes in the humanities, literature and the social sciences, particularly programmes in black studies and minority issues. Little attention was given to what processes should be included in these new curricular areas, just what content.

4. The final blow to this period of reform was the continued poor performance of American children on standardised mathematics and science tests. Unfortunately, as parents, politicians, and educators lamented the students' lack of ability to 'do' mathematics and science, few really examined what later was to be proven - the discrepancy between what was being taught in the classrooms under the guise of 'new' mathematics and science, and what was actually tested. Evaluation instruments were not redesigned quickly enough to adequately judge the quality and success of most of the new curricula programmes.

So America entered the 1970s, with the product-process debate placed on the 'back burner'. The emphasis during the 1970s, for most classrooms, was on minimum competencies. The public wanted to be reassured that all children were learning the 'essentials', reading, writing, and arithmetic. Accountability movements saw the inclusion of curriculum management programmes in many elementary schools, where the focus was on 'basic skills' acquisition. The cry in the 1970s was 'back to basics', enough of the exploratory and experimental 'fun' students had in the humanities, social sciences and literature classes during the tumultuous 1960s.

The current educational reform movement in the United States is spurred on by the numerous studies done in and about our public schools. In Goodlad's (1983) examination of schools he revealed that less than one per cent of teachers' interactions with students is devoted to the solicitation of open response from the students. Boyer (1983) found excessive attention to memorisation and recall of information and little concern for 'thinking' about what was being studied. National assessment results (1982) indicated that less than fifty per cent of our seventeen-year-old students could write persuasively, could apply mathematics successfully, could classify information accurately, or could analyse literature for mood. These scores were considerably lower than scores of similar students in 1975. (Costa, 1985) The conclusion drawn was 'the pattern is clear: the percentage of students achieving higher order skills is declining' (Education Commission of the States, 1982). The concern about what and how we are teaching our students is exacerbated by reports of poor performance by American students on science, mathematics, and geography tests given to students from various countries. Best selling books in the States have been Hirsch's *Cultural Literacy* (1987) and Bloom's *The Closing of the American Mind* (1987). And, a final warning is heard by the futurists (Naisbitt, 1982) who claim that tomorrow's basics are such skills as: evaluation, analysis, critical thinking, problem-solving, synthesis, application, decision-making, organisation of information, and communication through a variety of media; skills which many of America's children do not seem to exhibit in any testing or comparative data shared with the public.

As a result of all the concern and criticism, the product-process debate has been removed from the back burner and is being openly addressed by educators. However, process now is defined as higher order thinking skills (HOTS), and product refers to the results of the minimum competency curriculum. The central question of the debate is, 'How can HOTS, be effectively incorporated into the public schools curriculum?' Everyone agrees that more attention must be devoted to higher order thinking skills, but there is little consensus as to how to proceed. Sternberg (1984), Perkins (1984), and Beyer (1985) contend that effective instruction in thinking skills development will only occur if the skills are integrated into the existing content areas. With such integration comes the necessity of identifying for the students the higher order thinking skills they are using and helping them to analyse the skills so that they can transfer that knowledge to different situations at a later time. Beyer (1985) reports research results on thinking skill learning and teaching which suggest:

1. Teachers should provide students with opportunities to identify samples of a skill - or products of its use - before asking them to use the skills.

2. Skill components should be introduced as systematically as possible with specific emphasis on their basic attributes and procedural operations.

3. Students should frequently discuss skill operations and how to use them.

4. Thinking skills need to be practised over extended periods of time with corrective feedback provided by peers or teachers.

5. Skills need to be broadened beyond their original components and operations. Content specific examples should be introduced and combinations of skills should be emphasised.

6. To facilitate transfer, students need to apply and practise skills in a variety of settings and with a variety of data and media.

7. Teachers should present lessons using the thinking skills in content specific courses.

Reuven Fuererstein (1985), on the other hand, is not opposed to the integration of thinking skills into the existing content areas, but warns that if students do not possess the basic skills of thinking they cannot effectively use them in those integrated programmes. He advocates separate instruction in thinking skills development with emphasis on the teacher's ability to 'bridge' the skills to specific applications in content areas - when, and only when, the students have mastered the skills. Fuererstein does not stand alone. Others believe that special programmes can be designed to develop thinking skills. The American curriculum journals are inundated with advertisements for thinking skills programmes which are guaranteed to improve students' thinking skills. Prepackaged programmes are popular among administrators because they are easy enough to use and assure a consistency, so the administrators believe, of learning from classroom to classroom. Also, these types of programmes usually come with evaluation instruments which can be used to 'prove' learning of the thinking skills has taken place. However, finding time to introduce 'packaged learning' into an already crowded curriculum frustrates most teachers. In fact, such use of programmes conveys the idea that teachers have purposely neglected the teaching of thinking skills and need special materials to correct the oversight. Teachers have not intentionally ignored the teaching of thinking skills, they have just found it difficult to find the time to spend on these skills in light of the demands placed upon them to assure student progress in basic competencies, which are measured regularly in most school districts. So what can be done about the current product-process dilemma?

First, teachers must be convinced that the teaching of thinking skills can be *easily* integrated into their current curriculum. This convincing of teachers will only occur with proper in-service training, where teachers are exposed to a variety of ideas and approaches to how thinking skills can be taught. From these experiences, teachers should be allowed to select those strategies with which they can work and feel comfortable.

Second, teachers must be freed from the 'shackles' of basic skills accountability, and be allowed to organise and teach their curriculum as they deem appropriate for the age, ability, and interest levels of their students. Encouraging students to think about what they are learning will not make them less able to learn basic skills. In fact, the new emphasis might motivate students to learn the basics quicker.

Third, pre-service teachers must be trained to incorporate thinking skills strategies into their repertoire of teaching skills. They need to develop their own metacognitive skills with respect to the relationship between content and thinking. Many of these young people have not had the opportunity to effectively interact with the content they will be expected to teach, that is, they have learned to memorise and recall information rather than think about, critically analyse or question what they have been learning. The process of re-educating them may take considerable time and energy and cannot be done without the cooperation of all faculty members in the college/university setting. Colleges of education are not solely responsible for the content knowledge of teachers. Their responsibility rests with pedagogy and practical application (internships), not subject matter expertise (Kysilka and Davis, 1988).

Fourth, if schools deem it necessary to select 'thinking skills programmes', then the guidelines suggested by Sternberg (1983) should be followed:

1. The programme should be based on a psychological theory of the intellectual processes it seeks to train and on an educational theory of the way in which the processes will be taught.

2. The programme should be socioculturally appropriate. Programmes must relate to the cognitive structures and the real world of the students who will use the programmes.

3. The programme should provide explicit training both in the mental processes used in task performance and in self-management strategies for using these components.

4. The programme should be responsive to the motivational as well as the intellectual needs of the students.

5. The programme should be sensitive to individual differences. A programme which does not take into account these differences will surely fail.

6. The programme should provide explicit links between the training it provides and functioning in the real world. Transfer of training does not come easily. Without explicit examples, transfer is unlikely to occur.

7. Adoption of the programme should take into account demonstrated empirical success in implementations similar to one's own planned implementation. Just because a programme worked in one school is no guarantee it will work in all.

8. The programme should have associated with it a well-tested curriculum for teacher training. If teachers are insufficiently or improperly trained, the programme will surely fail.

9. Expectations should be appropriate for what the programme can accomplish.

Finally, the debate about product-process: what is effective learning? must be, once and for all, put to rest. Effective learning in any society is determined by what we measure according to the demands of our society. If product is what society wants and we teach for product and we measure product, then effective learning has taken place. If process is what is dictated and we teach process and measure process, then our students will have effectively learned and our society will be happy. However, as educators we must recognise that one cannot exist without the other and *we* ought to determine what *we* think is essential in this product-process marriage. What we teach our students of today must serve them well throughout their lifetimes. Our choices must be, not only timely, but characteristic of timelessness, for who knows what tomorrow brings?

References

Beyer, B. (1985) Teaching critical thinking: a direct approach, *Social Education* (49), 4, pp. 297-303.

Bloom, A. (1987) *The Closing of the American Mind*, Simon and Schuster, New York.

Boyer, E. (1983) *High School*, Harper and Row, New York.

Costa, A. (ed.) (1985) *Developing Minds: A Resource Book for Teaching Thinking*, Association for Supervision and Curriculum Development, Alexandria, VA.

Fuererstein, R. *et al.*, (1985) Instrumental enrichment: an intervention program for structural cognitive modifiability, in Segal *et al.* (eds), *Thinking and Learning Skills*, Volume 1, Erlbaum, Hillsdale, NJ.

Goodlad, J. (1983) *A Place Called School: Prospects for the Future*, McGraw Hill, New York.

Hirsch, E. (1987) *Cultural Literacy*, Houghton Mifflin Co., Boston.

Kysilka, M. and Davis, O. (1988) Teaching as thinking in action, in Wood *et al.* (eds), *Reading, Writing, and Thinking in Education*, Ginn Press, Needham Heights, MA.

Naisbitt, J. (1982) *Megatrends: Ten New Directions Transforming Our Lives*, Warner Books, New York.

Parker, J. and Rubin, L. (1966) *Process as Content*, Rand McNally and Co, Chicago.

Perkins, D. (1984) Creativity by design, *Educational Leadership*, (42), 1, pp. 18-24.

Sternberg, R. (1984) *How can we teach intelligence?*, *Educational Leadership*, (42), 1, pp. 38-48.

US Office of Education (1982) *Final Report National Assessment of Educational Progress* Education Commission of the States, Washington DC.

Chapter 13

Performance indicators for effective learning[1]

Carolyn Skilling and Alan Sutton

INTRODUCTION

Recently, various sectors of the education service, secondary, tertiary and higher education have been required to identify performance indicators to assist in the delivery of education and to make judgements on the effectiveness and efficiency of that provision. Performance indicators are being developed in a climate where there is increasing emphasis on demonstrating accountability.

The original guidance from the Department of Education and Science (DES) suggested an emphasis on performance indicators as measurable outcomes which would be used to compare institutions. However, there has been evidence of a move towards the use of indicators to provide evidence of change from year to year on various aspects of a school's performance.

Some educationalists see performance indicators as management tools which assist in improving effectiveness by managing organisational change. In this sense the emphasis is on the formative as opposed to the summative use of indicators, and may be linked with school development plans. Schools and colleges in Leicestershire are currently involved in a cycle of curriculum review to improve the quality of students' learning. As part of this cycle, schools and colleges are being asked to identify their own performance targets and indicators based on evolving guidelines from the local education authority. The cycle is also used as the basis for TVEI forward planning, implementation, monitoring and evaluation.

THE USE OF PERFORMANCE MEASUREMENT

Early DES literature on performance indicators clearly associated their use with raising educational standards and demonstrating increased accountability to client groups. The documents suggested that annual performance targets could be set by institutions for a range of activities which included examination results, attendance, truancy, lateness, participation rates post-sixteen, etc.

By employing measurable outcome indicators which were standardized, it would be possible to provide information to parents, governors and employers to aid them to make decisions on the effectiveness of institutions.

The approach of the Training Agency to the use of performance indicators can be seen in planning for work-related non-advanced further education, TVEI, compacts and the enterprise in higher education initiative. The Training Agency appear to be interested in indicators to provide evidence for what has actually changed in practice as a result of the injection of funding. Another approach to the use of performance indicators is that described in the 'joint efficiency study', *Managing Colleges Efficiently* (DES/LAA, 1988) which recommended the use of performance indicators to monitor students' movements through courses in further education. The recommended indicators were the ratio of:

- enrolled students over target enrolment;
- completions over enrolments;
- successful completions over completions;
- destinations.

In Leicestershire, performance targets and indicators are being set both to satisfy the demands for external accountability and to improve practice. A crucial aspect of the use of indicators is how to derive them and how to use the information for management and in the teaching/ learning situation. The framework for their use is the annual cycle of curriculum review and the context within this paper is the TVEI extension.

Within the curriculum review, performance targets and indicators are perceived as tools to manage change by requiring teachers to plan, phase and prioritize developments. For TVEI purposes, schools and colleges are required to set annual performance targets in relation to the LEA aims for TVEI extension. Examples are shown in Table 1 on TVEI and performance indicators.

Schools and colleges involved in TVEI and compacts will need to develop targets and indicators in relation to the transition to employment or further education and training. These may also need to be developed for records of achievement, work experience, guidance and counselling and equal opportunities.

The following example relates to records of achievement:

Performance target	**Outcome indicator**
To promote the use of records of achievement (ROA) by employers in the recruitment and selection of school leavers	Number of companies or per cent increase in the companies using records of achievement to recruit and select leavers

Performance indicators are also being developed to help to make judgements on the quality of the students' learning experience. A recent investigation of the planning and implementation of 'quality' work experience (Palmer, 1988),

Table 1: TVEI and performance indicators

TVEI aims	Possible form of TVEI delivery	Possible focus for development of PIs
Provide a broad, balanced, relevant and differentiated curriculum	Balanced science IT across the curriculum Technology across the curriculum	Balanced science
Active learning	LMF - Leicestershire Modular Framework GCSE CPVE BTEC ROA WE - work experience SSS - supported self-study IT	LMF SSS (A-level) IT
Prepare students for adult and working life	Work experience Enterprise Economic awareness	An experience of work pre- and post-sixteen enterprise
Value the full range of student achievement	Records of achievement (ROA)	Records of achievement (ROA) pre- and post-sixteen
Improve fourteen to nineteen progression	Guidance and counselling Links Records of achievement (ROA) EO - equal opportunities WE - work experience	Guidance and counselling - pre- and post-sixteen

based on case studies of selected schools, revealed that little formal attempt was being made to monitor and evaluate the experience. One particular difficulty was the failure of the schools to identify objectives in precise terms in order that performance indicators could be developed to establish the extent to which objectives had been met. Leicestershire local education authority policy guidelines for work experience recommend objectives, for example:

Objective	Exemplar performance indicator for outcome
To assist the student in choosing a future occupation	Students: Confirmed their suitability/ unsuitability for a particular job Refined their vocational choice to a broad vocational area Considered a career in an area in which they would not previously have contemplated as a result of work experience.

A current evaluation of the Leicestershire GCSE modular framework (Sutton *et al.*, 1990), which is focused on the students' learning experience, demonstrates the use of process indicators to provide evidence of progress in relation to objectives. An example is provided below which illustrates process indicators of a management type and also those for learning opportunities. This distinction is explained more fully later in the chapter.

Objective 1 of the evaluation	Performance indicator (process)
To investigate the use of the community as a learning resource	*Organisational* Have new timetabling arrangements been made to make it easier to use the community as a learning resource, for example, large blocks of time? Have arrangements been made to use industrialists in a consultancy capacity, for example, to help devise learning materials, to provide expert assistance, etc.?

> *Learning opportunities*
> Do the students have the
> opportunity to:
>
> complete assignments using
> authentic materials of contexts?
>
> visit local companies to enhance
> the learning experience?

In future it is likely that more emphasis will be placed on the use of process indicators for classroom-based evaluation.

THE USE OF PERFORMANCE TARGETS AND INDICATORS IN CURRICULUM REVIEW

Curriculum review cycle

Figure 1 is intended to demonstrate the role of performance targets and indicators within Leicestershire's curriculum review cycle. This process is important for the devising of development plans.

Aims for fourteen to nineteen education

In order to meet the contractual requirements of TVEI, local education authorities and schools and colleges have to demonstrate to the Training Agency the extent to which these broad aims are being implemented. TVEI aims, which are an integral part of fourteen to nineteen education, need to be more specific if they are to be the basis for planning, implementation, monitoring and evaluation. This can be achieved by the use of performance targets which are directly related to the aims, but are more specific.

Clarifying a rationale for performance targets which relates to a set of aims is likely to lead to a greater understanding and acceptance by teachers and lecturers of the need for change.

In setting performance targets, schools and colleges will need to identify a possible focus for development (see Table 1). This illustrates that performance targets for LEA aims can be identified for a variety of TVEI vehicles. It also demonstrates that specific vehicles can deliver a number of TVEI aims. For example, records of achievement can satisfy aims for active learning, preparing students for adult and working life, valuing the full range of student achievement and improving fourteen to nineteen progression. The school or college development plan will focus on local priorities as a result of carrying out a situational analysis and determining their principles for quality experience.

Performance targets can be set for courses, modular developments or experiences. In order to set performance targets, it may be necessary to produce more

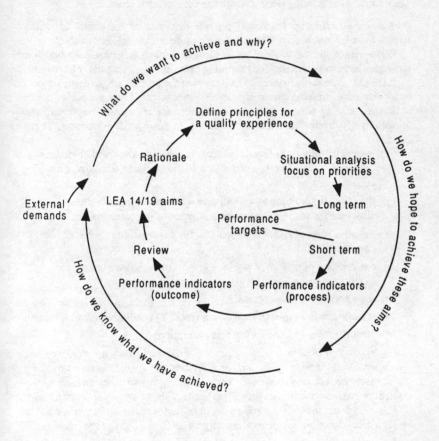

Figure 1: Curriculum review cycle

specific aims from those broad aims identified in a development plan. Performance targets are derived from these aims. It is possible to distinguish two types of performance indicator.

Process indicators are evidence that action has been taken in relation to targets. They show what is being done to facilitate the intended change.

Performance indicators (outcome) provide evidence of the extent to which targets have been achieved. These can be qualitative as well as quantitative.

Performance indicators need to be identified when targets are set because strategies have to be devised for recording them and for using the information.

It should be possible to identify indicators at the process stage which support or facilitate the implementation of a performance target. These are performance indicators relating to *management or organisational issues*. They entail the allocation of physical and human resources to support development. These include:

- the availability of policy documents identifying aims and objectives for specific TVEI cross-curricular initiatives, for example, records of achievement;
- the allocation of time to an initiative - this could include time allocated for planning purposes and time for implementation;
- the allocation of financial resources, for example, to purchase consumables;
- the creation of new staff working groups to facilitate change, for example, a record of achievement working party;
- the allocation of support staff;
- the allocation of in-service training (INSET) funding to development;
- arrangements for monitoring and evaluation.

It should also be possible to identify process indicators which are evidence that pupils have had *learning opportunities* in relation to the performance targets of the course, module or experience. These learning opportunities relate to the content or organisation of the curriculum and teaching/learning and assessment.

Progress made towards the achievement of performance targets will need to be reviewed, decisions taken and new targets set in the light of the evidence.

Characteristics of worthwhile targets and indicators

Recent evidence derived from the experience of schools and colleges, using performance targets and indicators in curriculum review, strongly suggests that clear guidelines need to be provided by local education authorities to assist in the setting of targets and the identification of indicators. It is suggested that if performance targets are to be effective, they should have the following characteristics:

- be challenging, but possible, in the time and with the resources available;
- be directly related to aims, but be more specific;
- be a realistic number which implies that decisions have been made about priorities;
- be written in clear concise and unambiguous language, so that it is possible to derive outcome indicators;
- be identified with staff who will have to implement them;
- take into consideration the readiness of the school or college to implement them.

Effective indicators are likely to have the following characteristics:

- be directly related to the target;
- be acceptable to the users, because judgements will be based on them;
- be a realistic number, because information needs to be collated and used;
- be written in clear simple language;
- be both quantitative and qualitative;
- be identified for the process as well as the outcome stage;
- it should be possible to provide evidence in support of the indicator.

MANAGEMENT ISSUES IN THE IDENTIFICATION AND USE OF TARGETS AND INDICATORS

Already, as a result of developmental work on performance targets and indicators in Leicestershire, a range of issues have emerged that need to be considered for those considering embarking on using targets and indicators. The use of performance targets and indicators needs to be an integral part of the management function of the school/college. Improving practice may be perceived as the priority area for the use of targets and indicators, but if more emphasis is to be placed on providing information to the public, there is a need to clarify the information which is made available to the community.

There is clearly a need to clarify terminology in relation to performance measurement. In particular, terms such as monitoring, evaluation, assessment and review are often used interchangeably. In the context of Leicestershire's curriculum review, the following distinctions are made:

Monitoring   means collecting relevant information or evidence, for example, by observation.

Assessment   will refer only to measuring or describing children's achievements.

(Formative) implies making (continual) informed judgements about worth-
Evaluation   whileness, based on feedback from monitoring and assessment.

Review   means reflecting on decisions, policies and plans in the light of
             all the above.

In devising school/college development plans, there is a need to make an explicit link between aims, targets, process and outcome indicators. This is the recommended sequence for the identification of targets and indicators.

Target-setting is a critical stage for improving performance. Confusion between aims and targets is common; some teachers and lecturers may find it difficult to write clear, concise targets. As the setting of targets needs to be done in consultation with those who will have to implement them, there is a need to create time for this process.

It should be possible to record information in a manner which does not create too much extra pressure. Some of the information should be already available, otherwise changes in practice will need to be made to make the evidence available.

Many so called 'indicators' produced by schools and colleges have been vague statements, sometimes related to targets but often not. Much work remains to be done to identify indicators, qualitative or quantitative, which are specific, valid and useful. In spite of external pressure to identify outcome indicators which are quantitative, these may say little about the quality of the learning experience.

The cyclical process of curriculum review encourages teachers and lecturers to reflect on their experience and form personal judgements. The process of setting targets and analysing performance, using previously defined performance indicators, adds rigour to the exercise of review. Teachers/lecturers are thus able to make a visible and personal contribution to the improvement of quality of educational experiences.

Note

1. The substance of this chapter has been reworked as a practical guideline for schools and colleges in Leicestershire as: Gann, S., Jewitt, M., Mayne, P., Skilling, C., Smith, J. and Sutton, A. (1990) *Performance Targets and Indicators in School/College Development Planning*.

References

DES/LAA (1988) *Managing Colleges Efficiently. A report of a study of efficiency in non-advanced further education for the government and the local authorities association.*

Palmer, A. (1988) *Evaluation of Work Experience in a Selection of Leicestershire Schools*, Public Sector Economic Research Centre, University of Leicester.

Sutton, A. *et al.* (1990) *Evaluation of the Leicestershire Modular Framework: The Student Experience.*

Further reading

There is a useful and extensive bibliography of school evaluation and performance indicators in: Thomas, H., Kirkpatrick, G. & Nicholson, E. (1989) *Financial Delegation and the Local Management of Schools: Preparing for Practice*, pp. 171-173.

The following have been particularly helpful in preparing this paper:DES (1988) *Performance Indicators: Some Practical Considerations.*Wakefield, B. (1988) Performance indicators in secondary schools: some practical considerations, in *Quality in Schools: A Briefing Conference* held on 29 June 1988, Queen Elizabeth II Conference Centre, NFER.

Contributors

Michael Armstrong: Headteacher, Harwell Primary School, Oxfordshire

Tim Brighouse: Professor of Education, Keele University, formerly Chief Education Officer, Oxfordshire

O L Davis Jnr.: Professor of Curriculum and Instruction, University of Texas

Tim Everton: Senior Lecturer in Education, Leicester University

Alec Fisher: Department of Philosophy, University of East Anglia

Maurice Galton: Professor of Education, Leicester University

Marcella Kysilka: Professor Educational Foundations, University of Central Florida

Peter Mayne: Vice Principal, Rutland Sixth Form College, Oakham, Leicestershire

Bob Moon: Professor of Education, Open University

Stephen Munby: General Adviser/Inspector (Assessment and Testing) Oldham MBC

Joan Sallis: Chair of the Campaign for the Advancement of State Education and Chair of the Action for Governors Education and Training

Eleanor Scheirer: University of North Florida

Brian Simon: Professor Emeritus, Leicester University

Carolyn Skilling: County 14-19 Adviser (TVEI), Leicestershire

Alan Sutton: Leicester University School of Education

Steve White: Headteacher, Rushey Mead School, Leicester

Keith Wood-Allum: Director of Education, Leicestershire

Cecile Wright: Leicester University School of Education